METAVERSE

*The Ultimate Guide to Investing in Virtual Lands,
NFT (Crypto Art), Altcoins, and Cryptocurrency
Using Blockchain Technology
(2022 Crash Course for Beginners)*

Rufus Hudson

1

TABLE OF CONTENTS

INTRODUCTION

Even before Facebook was renamed Meta, the concept of "the metaverse" was alive and well, and CEO Mark Zuckerberg spoke extensively about it. There's no getting around it: the metaverse has arrived, and it's here to stay.

So, exactly what is the metaverse? Is it as important as some corporations claim, or is it just a fad that will pass in a few months? Is it necessary to know everything there is to know about the metaverse, and should you get involved before it explodes? This book delves into the concept of the metaverse, discussing its past, present, and, most importantly, future.

CHAPTER 1

THE METAVERSE CONCEPT

Despite its youth, the metaverse appears to be everywhere. The recent rebranding and investments by Facebook, er, Meta, have sparked renewed interest in the metaverse. It's everywhere in the news, memes, gaming platforms, and social media. The term's growing popularity creates a sense of impending doom as if our physical lives will be enveloped at any moment, incorporating pixels and paywalled exchanges. However, games such as Fortnite and Roblox have been promoting the metaverse for years, and the term itself is decades old.

So, exactly what is the metaverse?

Mark Zuckerburg's rendition conjures up a virtual reality vision: You use the Quest VR headset as an avatar to attend business meetings and a device on your wrist to secretly text friends. When you go outside, you'll put on smart glasses that record what you see and hear and provide augmented reality. Phones, laptops, wearable technology, and headsets will be able to access the metaverse (or a combination of these). It will be your workspace, where you will work, exercise, shop, socialise, watch movies, and play video games.

However, the term predates much of the technology that may enable it to become a reality. The suffix meta- can mean "beyond or beyond," "more extensive," or even "transformative" (as in metamorphosis). The term "-verse" is derived from the word "universe" and can refer to a specific sphere or area (such as the Twitterverse) or a fictitious world (such as the omegaverse (sorry!), a speculative alternate reality literary genre in which characters are divided into alphas, betas, and omegas). A "metaverse" is a virtual environment that exists outside, on top of, or in addition to the real world.

The term was first used in Neal Stephenson's 1992 dystopian sci-fi novel Snow Crash. According to the novel, the Metaverse is a collection of virtual and augmented realities centred on a super-long "Street" that people can walk across as avatars and access via goggles and computers. Users of public terminals are represented by a fuzzy black and white avatar, whereas users of private terminals are represented in full colour and detail. Since then, the term "metaverse" has come to refer to a wide range of activities aimed at creating a more permanent virtual world that pervades our everyday lives.

People have been attempting to create immersive virtual worlds since the 1960s, a desire fueled by the efforts of the film and video game industries. Second Life, an alt-reality computer game in which you control an avatar and may do anything you want, such as buy a house or get married, was released in 2003 and is one of the most well-known examples of the metaverse. There was even a thriving kink culture in such a realistic environment — it doesn't get any more realistic than that. Nonetheless, by 2006, there were enough dedicated metaverse specialists to convene a summit.

The Metaverse Roadmap, a project that mapped the path to metaverse completion, arose from that summit. According to the Metaverse Roadmap, "the merging of virtually-enhanced physical reality with [a] physically persistent virtual realm." In other words, it may resemble a second world superimposed over our own via augmented reality, as well as a virtual area into which we can enter and exit, similar to the video game in Spy Kids 3. Consider Snapchat filters or the Google function for viewing life-size 3D animal models. According to the Metaverse Roadmap, "the Metaverse would not be the entirety of the Internet–but, like the Web, it would be seen by many as the most significant element."

Many of today's evangelists would claim that we now have the technology, protocols, and infrastructure in place to step on the gas and make it happen for the first time. It is thought to be the next logical step after mobile internet. The metaverse investigates virtual reality, Zoom meetings, augmented reality, social networks, crypto, NFTs, online retail, wearable tech, artificial intelligence, 5G, and other topics. It's predicted to be the future! Because the future cannot be avoided, it must be positive, right?

Many of those extolling the virtues of the metaverse and arguing that it is the natural next step is Silicon Valley voices, futurists (the Metaverse Roadmap's John Smart), and other players with a financial stake in its realisation. Mark Zuckerberg is undoubtedly one of them. "...a vast network of 3D environments and simulations rendered in real-time."

According to Ball, the metaverse is "a vast network of persistent, real-time generated 3D environments and simulations." Ball's metaverse should retain identity, objects, history, and payments continuity. It should be felt by an infinite number of people at the same time, with each person having their own sense of presence. The metaverse is a persistent virtual world that allows people to be present, and it's a place where blockchain technology could be used to pay for things we can bring with us through various experiences:

Consider using your Animal Crossing Sandy Liang fleece in your Twitter and Instagram profile photos. Ball's metaverse is constantly expanding and changing.

Ball's metaverse has a significant impact on Zuckerberg's.

In his Facebook Connect presentation, Zuckerberg's avatar moved from platform to platform, wearing the same black t-shirt to demonstrate "continuity of identity and things."

With nearly 3 billion Facebook users, Zuckerberg's metaverse is well on its way to housing an infinite number of people. Throughout his presentation, Zuckerberg emphasized the importance of each aspect of the metaverse in creating a "feeling of presence."

These days, Roblox and Epic Games' Fortnite is frequently mentioned in metaverse discussions, and some argue that they are much closer to realising the metaverse than Zuckerberg's Meta. This is due to the fact that both games meet the criteria for persistent virtual worlds: they each have millions of players who come to play and socialize, there is some persistence in things (clothing and skins), and payment is accepted (Robux and V-Bucks). Furthermore, millions of people watched Ariana Grande's performance in Fortnite, and these events, along with customizable avatars and emotes, are creating a sense of "presence."

The most crucial concept to understand is that the metaverse does not exist. Like many other investors, engineers, scientists, and futurists, Zuckerberg has stated that the metaverse is a long-term goal for him. People, of course, despise Zuckerberg's proposal, and there is no faith in Meta's metaverse's ability to do anything other than incalculable harm, to the point of labelling it a dystopian catastrophe. Nonetheless, the metaverse is an idea — one that excites some and terrifies others.

Rhizome, a nonprofit art organisation leading efforts to archive digital art and culture, hosted the Welcome to the Metaverse conference. According to artist David Rudnick, "the notion of the metaverse is the ultimate centralization," which contradicts many of the hopes for democratisation we once had for the internet. "When people talk about the emergent metaverse dream," Rudnick explains, "they're talking about a space where you'll be able to do everything [in a virtual world]," a commercial public space "that can extract value or some sort of ownership from all of the interactions that take place on the platform."

Fears and concerns about the metaverse are fundamentally about scale. Any increase in the negative aspects of the virtual world is likely to exacerbate them. What does it mean if a few for-profit corporations mediate so many critical interactions? If Meta's current social media dominance is any indication, there isn't much reason to be hopeful.

Governments have a history of being slow to comprehend, let alone regulate, technological advances.

Can a government that has no idea what a finsta is be trusted to keep the metaverse safe, ethical, and sustainable? What are the human and environmental costs and benefits if this is pursued?

For the time being, the metaverse is mostly fiction, a hypothesis, and fantasy, with plenty of open spaces for the icy winds of the unknown to blow through.

What exactly is the metaverse, and how does it function? An in-depth examination of the "future of the internet."

The metaverse is a type of virtual reality.

Original Series: What's Next? Image of the Day

The metaverse is a virtual world, but it is not like what you've seen in science fiction movies.

Consider The Matrix, in which the world is a digital simulation to which everyone is connected and which is so well-crafted that almost no one realises it isn't real. The metaverse isn't there yet, but it has the potential to be spectacularly immersive.

The concept of the metaverse is much older than Meta's conception of it; in fact, it predates even Facebook. "An embodied internet that you're inside of rather than just looking at," Zuckerberg said.

The true definition of the metaverse is as hazy as Zuckerberg's.

At its most basic, the metaverse is a virtual environment in which people from all over the world can interact with one another and with the metaverse itself. Users can frequently

13

collect objects and keep them between sessions, or they can even land in the metaverse. That concept, however, can be interpreted in a variety of ways, and it has evolved significantly over time.

We are constantly interacting with something on the internet, whether it is a website, a game, or chat software that connects us to our friends. The metaverse expands on this by immersing the user in action. This allows for more powerful, lifelike experiences that are rarely if ever, elicited by simply browsing the web or watching a video.

What exactly is the difference between virtual reality and the metaverse?

Although both virtual reality (VR) and augmented reality (AR) is related to the metaverse, they are not the same thing. Instead, think of them as distinct entities that complement one another rather than different incarnations of essentially the same entity.

Using VR and AR technology, the user can immerse himself in a virtual environment. In the case of virtual reality, we are presented with entirely different environments. VR, whether through a game or a movie, allows you to interact with the changing world around you. AR, on the other hand, adds objects to your real-world environment and allows you to interact with them in a variety of ways.

A virtual reality headset is being worn by a person.

The difference is in the goal. You can play a VR or AR game without ever connecting with others, but the human touch is the cornerstone of the metaverse, as Meta and other companies envision.

In a nutshell, the metaverse is a playground for both of the aforementioned — a way for individuals to share a virtual environment for business, study, fitness, or simply for fun.

The use of virtual reality and augmented reality tools will help to expand the metaverse and make it feel more real than a video game with extra steps. The metaverse, on the other hand, is supposed to bring people closer together in previously unimaginable ways, not just through VR and AR. As a result, there is plenty of room for expansion.

Who or what is building the metaverse?

Because of Zuckerberg's recent Meta address, millions of new eyes have been drawn to the metaverse, but there are numerous titans in this race to the future. Furthermore, each of these businesses interprets the metaverse, adding to the term's already broad definition.

Facebook's entry into the metaverse isn't entirely surprising. In March 2014, Facebook paid $2.3 billion for Oculus. The company continued to release Oculus Quest devices, which are among the best virtual reality headsets available today.

Given that Meta intends to rely heavily on both VR and AR to add realism to the metaverse, purchasing Oculus seven years ago does not appear to be a random decision. It's worth noting that Oculus Quest will be phased out soon. Beginning in 2022, the entire product line will be rebranded as Meta Quest, bringing the transaction to a close and removing the old branding.

Aside from Meta Quest, Meta's chief technology officer Andrew Bosworth revealed that some Oculus products will be dubbed Meta Horizon. This will be the branding for the entire virtual reality metaverse platform, according to Bosworth.

In front of a grey background, a person is wearing an Oculus Quest 2 VR headset.

Oculus.com/Facebook

With Facebook's big announcement out in the open, Microsoft quickly jumped aboard the metaverse bandwagon. Microsoft intends to launch a metaverse within Microsoft Teams in 2022.

Microsoft plans to use Mesh to replace webcam photos with animated avatars in video meetings, allowing all Teams users to participate. Listening to the user's voice, artificial intelligence will animate their avatar with matching lip movements. Switching to 3D meetings will also result in more hand movements.

While Microsoft's statement may appear insignificant in comparison to Meta's, it is a significant step toward the metaverse that shows the company's commitment.

Furthermore, as evidenced by these updates to Teams, Microsoft, like Meta, may intend to integrate the metaverse into the future of remote work.

The Nvidia Omniverse is yet another horse in Nvidia's metaverse race. It was described by the company as "a platform for integrating 3D environments into a shared virtual cosmos." Nvidia's Omniverse is cloud-native, which means it's a shared, persistent platform that stays the same between sessions. It can also be streamed remotely to any device and is compatible with RTX-based platforms.

Omniverse Replicator Applications

So far, it appears that the graphics card behemoth has taken a slightly different approach to its metaverse. While Meta and Microsoft emphasise the social aspects of the metaverse, Nvidia focuses on collaboration and the exploration of new technologies. Designers, robotics engineers, and other experts use the Omniverse to create virtual reality simulations of the real world. Ericsson engineers, for example, use Omniverse to simulate 5G waves in urban environments.

In terms of the future, another big-ticket player is on the way. Apple is developing full virtual reality headgear as well as augmented reality glasses, and all signs point to the company heading towards the metaverse. Both of these products would almost certainly require a connection to a metaverse in order to function; thus, Apple may not be far behind Meta in terms of metaverse development.

Is the metaverse just a stage for a video game?

Short answer: I don't believe so.

Long answer: Depending on your perspective, maybe a little.

All online games, including Fortnite, World of Warcraft, and Minecraft, have their own metaverses. They create a permanent environment in which their players can come and go as they please. Furthermore, a player's progress is saved on an external server and shared with other users, so anything you do in these games can be reviewed later.

Every game is technically a metaverse, and the metaverses that various tech behemoths are developing may all include gaming elements. The metaverse concept, on the other hand, is much broader than that of a video game. The metaverse is designed to replace or improve real-world functionality in a virtual environment. Things that users do on a daily basis, such as going to class or working, are all possible in the metaverse.

There are some parallels between video game metaverses and the concept of a larger metaverse. You can, for example, communicate with others, collaborate on various activities, and even change the world around you to some extent. However, all of this is constrained by the game's constraints.

In Minecraft, for example, you can build a massive fortress; however, in World of Warcraft, you don't have the same level of freedom. Players can instead own a garrison, which is essentially a plot of land, though they have little to no control over how it looks or where it is placed. More importantly, all players are involved in the same plot and can only visit each other if they are invited.

This Minecraft project includes buildings and terrain.

Although the above-mentioned titles are currently popular, the concept of the metaverse can be found in many video games and has been around for quite some time.

Second Life, a 2003 game that is still active today, is a metaverse that, unlike many other games, does not have an end goal: it simply allows you to travel the world and communicate with other people. You can, by the way, fly.

Many traditional video game constraints are removed in an ideal metaverse, and you create your destiny. Regardless of whether you're in a game-related metaverse or not, the first step is always the same: you must create your character.

Changing into an avatar

Users in the metaverse are given an avatar that represents themselves and can be customised to their liking. The avatar's appearance is determined by the platform. It can be very basic, but it can also be very high quality, with numerous customization options. Users, for example, can remain loyal while potentially transforming into someone completely different.

Once created, the avatar serves as the user's ticket to the metaverse, a virtual world in which anything is possible if one has the imagination to suspend reality for a short period of time. Among other things, the avatar can walk, communicate, and explore the environment. However, the platform is solely to blame for the avatar's limitations.

There are four avatars in the Meta Horizon Worlds metaverse.

Some metaverse instances are designed to look like video games and allow users to move around by using a keyboard and mouse.

In more advanced versions, virtual reality headsets and controls are used to immerse the user in the scenario by simulating their real-life movements in the metaverse.

Depending on the company, the process of creating an avatar varies. Microsoft Mesh will be integrated into Teams in 2022, bringing something new to the metaverse. Using the application, the user will create a fully personalised avatar of himself. The avatar will be a realistic representation of the user thanks to mixed reality technologies. In the future, this will include a wide range of facial expressions, body language, and backgrounds.

Meta has great ideas for avatar creation in its next metaverse, Horizon Worlds. Avatars, which will mirror the user's activities in real-time, will be supported by virtual reality.

While this all sounds wonderful, these avatars do not currently have legs, possibly to make movement and travel easier. Meta is also working on photorealistic Codec Avatars, which are stunningly realistic avatars rendered in real-time with their surroundings.

When supported by VR, the ideal metaverse, regardless of platform, will allow users to choose how they want to appear while maintaining the realism of facial expressions and movements.

How does the metaverse manifest itself?

To begin answering this question, we must distinguish between "the metaverse" and "a metaverse." No single metaverse connects all other universes into a unified whole, despite the fact that they all use the internet to connect their users. As a result, each metaverse may have its own appearance.

A metaverse's appearance is determined by its creator. Some metaverses are sandbox-like, with a plethora of development opportunities and few constraints on what users can create. Consider Minecraft, but much larger: instead of sharing a server with friends, everyone lives in the same universe.

21

A metaverse can take the shape of a school, a street, a fantasy forest, or the depths of the ocean.

In such a metaverse, real-world rules still apply.

You will most likely see the sky, buildings, nature, and other people. The art style can be cartoony, realistic, or anything in between, depending on the metaverse.

The metaverse, on the other hand, does not have the same constraints as the real world, as Zuckerberg pointed out during his Meta speech. So, for example, there's no reason you couldn't travel to space with your entire family in the metaverse if the metaverse's creators permitted it.

To summarise, a metaverse can be likened to a school, a street, a dream forest, or the depths of the ocean. The most popular examples, on the other hand, provide a mix of those things due to the freedom they give their users.

Is it possible to build a metaverse?

Let's take a moment to assess where we are right now. First, we have virtual reality, in which the creator is the only one who has the ability to limit it. To represent ourselves, we've created an avatar. Then, of course, we have internet access, which allows us to be a part of this global community.

What are our next steps? It is conditional.

A metaverse vision featuring a slew of figures pointing to a future world.

In an ideal world, the metaverse would connect every single person. When you connect to a public server, you should be able to communicate with everyone else who is online at the same time. The truth, on the other hand, is frequently contradictory.

As the popularity of certain metaverses grows, the servers that host them become unable to handle the increased traffic. Some programmers create different layers that divide users, reducing the universe's size.

This may be avoided in the future, but for the time being, the metaverse is frequently fragmented — not to mention that people use multiple platforms, effectively choosing their favorite realm.

As previously stated, each company has its own point of view on the metaverse. For example, Facebook is developing Horizon Worlds, Nvidia is developing Omniverse, and much smaller fish are also participating in this very large pond.

Furthermore, the Bitcoin industry has its own metaverses.

The concept of a single massive metaverse is now unfeasible because different metaverses are isolated from one another, operate on different platforms, and have no shared uses or goals.

If the metaverse is one large, shared virtual environment, all enterprises releasing their metaverses will have to collaborate. Not only would these companies have to collaborate, but server technology would have to advance quickly as well.

To host all of these multiple iterations of the metaverse on one platform, the host and end-user would have to handle unimaginable server loads.

Until this is accomplished, the metaverse may remain fractured, requiring users to choose their preferred universe before connecting to the common world.

What is the purpose of the metaverse?

The concept of the metaverse is difficult to define, if only because it appears infinite. This, however, means that the organisation or group of individuals who created it, as well as each user, can define its general-purpose on an individual basis.

The metaverse's overarching goal is to bring people together by creating a virtual, shared universe. The metaverse exists to bridge the gap between reality and distance, bringing people from all over the world together for work, self-improvement, or simply entertainment.

Allowing users to interact with the world through their avatars without assigning them any specific purpose allows for a lot of freedom of choice. This is also the foundation of Meta's big reveal: the idea that you can do pretty much whatever you want in the metaverse.

Let's take a look at some of the more popular metaverse activities.

Possess property

Allowing people to buy land plots is a common theme in metaverses. When a user purchases a property, it is assigned to that user and is inaccessible to other players for the duration of that avatar's ownership. Just like in the real world, plots can be purchased or rented.

When you own property, you often have the freedom to do whatever you want with it. Some people, for example, prefer to open a gallery to display their possessions, whereas others open stores or create shared public areas.

Allowing users to build whatever they want in their environment isn't a new concept, and it's a big reason why games like Minecraft and Roblox are so popular. The developers of the metaverse save a lot of time by allowing users to create their own buildings, which would otherwise take a long time.

Of course, this is the internet, and too much freedom can lead to all sorts of problems. Most metaverses continue to monitor user-generated content, which may be removed depending on the host. Even the ostensibly infinite universe has limits.

Commercial property

You can sell or trade items you've acquired in the metaverse with other users. This adds a sense of wealth and prestige to an otherwise bleak world. Some lots are more valuable than others, and some are scarce while others are plentiful – all of this contributes to the development of a metaverse-specific economy.

The size and location of land plots in the metaverse vary. Given that the metaverse is a virtual representation of real life, it's no surprise that the real estate market is thriving. Contested plots that are closer to busy areas or are simply more desirable due to some other luxury can command far higher prices than a modest square of grass on the outskirts of town.

Decentraland is a metaverse based on blockchain technology.

Some metaverses are popular with both businesses and regular users. Because there are so many people who share the universe, it provides an opportunity to advertise.

Purchasing land and displaying the company's logo could be an effective way to generate or renew interest.

The metaverse can help businesses in a variety of ways. For example, in a seemingly limitless universe, it is easier to organise events, develop crossovers between properties, and communicate with the user community.

Interact and live

The previous examples of what you can accomplish in the metaverse are merely technicalities in comparison to the ideal metaverse- a realm capable of replacing reality.

We're not there yet (and probably won't be for years), but companies like Meta and VRChat are bringing us closer than ever.

You would interact with everyone in the vicinity in an ideal metaverse. This is more sophisticated than the text-based conversations seen in games like Second Life or Habbo. However, using voice communication, VR headsets, and AR glasses, interaction can be taken to a new level.

The metaverse's central premise will always be human interaction - but not in person. Whether it's meeting up with friends and skydiving or organizing a study group in a virtual library.

Work and education

Many companies, from Meta to Microsoft, place a high value on the ability to collaborate, study, and work together in the metaverse.

Microsoft intends to use Mesh to add realism to otherwise dull video sessions. Furthermore, meta aspires to build virtual workspaces that will allow remote workers to spend time together in virtual reality during the day.

Work can be done in a variety of ways in the metaverse, including first simulating real-world tasks in virtual reality.

Engineers, programmers, designers, and other professionals, for example, can use metaverses such as Nvidia's Omniverse to do so.

The metaverse, cryptocurrencies, and NFTs are all in some way linked.

It's difficult to discuss the metaverse without mentioning Bitcoin. After all, the blockchain, a decentralized foundation upon which cryptocurrencies operate, is used in some of the most well-known examples.

Decentraland, for example, is a sandbox-style metaverse where users can own land plots, explore other plots, and communicate. The MANA cryptocurrency, which is only used in Decentraland, serves as the foundation of the entire economy.

These metaverses are distinct from commercially owned universes in that they rely on a decentralized network in which your assets are your own and not controlled by the metaverse's owner (s).

Cryptocurrencies, like the worlds they inhabit, are almost always decentralized . This means that no single entity controls the currency, virtual land, or the entire metaverse, and thus it can never be taken down, sold, or otherwise destroyed.

Contracts are distributed to a network of users, and decentralisation is accomplished through a majority vote. Unless the majority of the network decides to shut it down, the metaverse should theoretically remain open to all.

This is not the case in gaming metaverses such as World of Warcraft, where your account remains the property of the game's creators. Regrettably, this means you don't have complete control over your assets, such as characters or equipment. This problem can be solved with NFTs (non-fungible tokens).

NFTs can be anything from 8-pixel avatars to incredible works of art (in my opinion, rather ugly). NFTs are, at their core, a decentralized system for granting ownership to virtual objects. NFTs use bitcoin and contracts to assign ownership to a specific user, whereas anyone can download a snapshot and claim ownership.

This adds a whole new level of the economy to the metaverse, transforming this fantastical concept into a way for people to make (or lose) real-world money. Users can use cryptocurrency to purchase virtual parcels of land, avatars, and even a hat for their metaverse avatar.

Non-fungible tokens concept, crypto art, NFT neon sign illustration on circuit board

Non-fungible tokens are not metaverse-dependent, but they do play a role in the economies of some universes that are still in development, such as Decentraland and The Sandbox.

The Sandbox sells NFTs, which give the customer full ownership of a plot of land. Users can then navigate to that visualisation and interact with the data contained within it. A quick glance at The Sandbox's map reveals that this type of NFT has piqued the interest of dozens of companies interested in exploring a new advertising area, not just bitcoin enthusiasts.

Several well-known companies and franchises have already purchased land in The Sandbox in advance of its official opening. Atari, The Walking Dead, RollerCoaster Tycoon, Shaun the Sheep, and even South China Morning Post feature vast swaths of land.

Although no one would accuse this group of companies of being particularly interested in NFTs or the metaverse, the concept does have value. Some businesses are attempting to capitalise on it.

It's difficult not to see parallels between how the bitcoin market interacts with some of the most popular metaverses and how the real-world economy functions. Depending on which side of the fence you're on, the end result could be fantastic or terrifying.

The Metaverse's Future

Nobody can deny that the metaverse concept has begun to expand into previously uncharted territory. We've come a long way since our humble beginnings in games like Second

Life, Habbo Hotel, and even the long-gone, long-forgotten Club Penguin.

According to Zuckerberg, meta intends to hit the ground running with Horizon Worlds, though even he admits that we're not there yet. The metaverse will take years to pervade our reality to the point where it is as well-known and accessible as Meta desires.

The metaverse's concept of a shared reality in which people from various continents can play, study, exchange, and even work together is futuristic and utopian. In the metaverse, bustling streets with shops, parks, and people can all be replicated, but the technology required to do so is still beyond the average person's reach.

The reality of the metaverse experience is a step closer to widespread acceptance. The incorporation of virtual and augmented reality into the metaverse will undoubtedly make the experience feel far more realistic than it does with a keyboard and mouse.

A screenshot from Travis Scott's Fortnite concert.

We've already seen some intriguing crossovers that pushed the boundaries of the metaverse. Travis Scott performed a virtual concert in Fortnite, which attracted over 12 million players.

Justin Bieber recently announced his intention to do the same.

Snoop Dogg, an outspoken supporter of NFTs, owns land in The Sandbox and allows visitors to purchase VIP passes to see his future home, even if it isn't yet open.

Zuckerberg sees the metaverse as the future of the internet, even referring to it as the "successor" to mobile internet. It remains to be seen whether this is correct.

One thing is certain: the metaverse is no longer a fantastical concept plucked from a science fiction movie.

Instead, Facebook/Meta has simply added fuel to an already raging fire, and in a few years, we may see the metaverse used in ways we never imagined possible.

WHO ELSE IS ABLE TO CREATE THE METAVERSE?

Although the Metaverse has the potential to replace the Internet as a computing platform, it is unlikely to follow in the footsteps of its forerunner. Public research universities and government programmes in the United States helped to develop the Internet. This was due in part to the fact that few in the private sector recognised the commercial potential of the World Wide Web. However, it was also due to the fact that these organisations were virtually the only ones with the computational power, resources, and goals to build it.

Unfortunately, none of this holds true in the Metaverse.

Private industry is not only fully aware of the Metaverse's potential, but it is also the most aggressive in its pursuit of it. The most money (at least when it comes from a willingness to support Metaverse research and development), the best engineering skill, and the most conquest ambition. Instead of simply leading the Metaverse, the major technology companies want to own and define it. Despite the fact that there are only a few potential leaders in the early Metaverse, open-source initiatives with a noncorporate approach will continue to play an important role.

They will be able to attract some of the most intriguing creative talents. And you'll be able to distinguish between them.

Microsoft is a great example of this. The company has hundreds of millions of federated user identities via Office 365 and LinkedIn, is the world's second-largest cloud vendor, has a comprehensive suite of work-related software and services spanning all systems/platforms/infrastructure, clear technical experience in massive shared online content/operations, and a set of potential gateway experiences via Minecraft, Xbox + Xbox Live, and HoloLens. To that end, the Metaverse allows Microsoft to reclaim the OS/hardware leadership it lost during the PC-to-mobile transition. But, more importantly, Microsoft CEO Satya Nadella recognises the value of being present wherever work is done. Microsoft has successfully transitioned from business to consumer, from PC to mobile, and from offline to online, all while maintaining a strong presence in the "work" economy. As a result, it's difficult to imagine Microsoft not playing a key role in the virtualized future of labour and information processing.

Although Facebook CEO Mark Zuckerberg has not explicitly stated his desire to create and control the Metaverse, his interest in it is obvious. This is also clever.

Facebook stands to lose the most from the Metaverse, as it will develop a new computing and interaction platform, as well as a larger and more capable social network. Simultaneously, the Metaverse enables Facebook to expand its reach both up and down the stack. Despite numerous attempts to create a smartphone operating system and consumer hardware, Facebook is the only FAAMG company that is solely focused on the app/service layer. Because of the Metaverse, Facebook could become the next Android or iOS/iPhone (hence Oculus) and Amazon's virtual goods counterpart.

The benefits of Facebook's Metaverse are enormous. It has the most daily users, daily usage, and usergenerated content of any platform on the planet, as well as the second-highest percentage of digital ad spend, billions of dollars, thousands of world-class engineers, and a founder with majority voting rights. Its Metaverse assets are also evolving quickly, with semiconductor patents and brain-to-machine computing interfaces now among them.

Unfortunately, Facebook's track record as a platform that allows third-party developers/companies to build long-term enterprises, as a ringleader in a consortium (e.g. Libra), and in managing user data/trust is dismal.

Amazon is fascinating in many ways. Of course, it will strive to be the primary location where we buy'stuff.' It makes no difference whether it is purchased via a game engine, a virtual environment, or a web browser (it already sells inside Twitch). Furthermore, the company already has hundreds of millions of credit cards, the world's largest share of ecommerce (excluding China), is the world's largest cloud vendor, operates a variety of consumer media experiences (video, music, ebooks, audiobooks, video game broadcasting, and so on) and third-party commerce platforms (e.g. Fulfilled by Amazon, Amazon Channels), and is working on what they hope will be the first major gaming/rendering engine purpose-built for the cloud.

More importantly, the company's founder and CEO, Jeff Bezos, believes strongly in infrastructure investment. AWS, for example, serves as the backbone of the internet (Amazon Web Services).

Rather than directly buying and selling inventory, Amazon sells, packages, and distributes products offered by other companies, with "Fulfilled by Amazon" accounting for 80% of Amazon's revenue (like most retailers). While Elon Musk's private rocket company, SpaceX, seeks to populate Mars, Bezos has stated that his goal with Blue Origin is to "create giant chip factories in orbit and just send small pieces down," similar to early web protocols and his AWS. As a result, Amazon is more likely than any other FAAMG company to embrace a fully "open" Metaverse — it doesn't need to control the UX or ID because of massive growth in back-end infrastructure usage and digital transactions.

The Internet is a data gold mine, and the Metaverse will have more data and potentially higher yields than the current web. And no one does a better job of exploiting this data on a global scale than Google. Furthermore, not only is the company the industry leader in indexing both the digital and physical worlds (nearly 10,000 employees contribute to mapping operations), but it is also the most successful digital software and services company outside of China. It also runs the world's most popular operating system (Android) and is the most open of the major consumer computing platforms (Windows). Despite its failure, Google Glass was the first to go all-in on wearable computing. With Google Assistant, its Nest suite of products, and FitBit, it is now making a significant push into digitising the home. As a result, the Metaverse is likely to be the

34

only project capable of bringing together all of Google's current investments, including Stadia edge computing, Project Fi, Google Street View, massive dark fibre purchases, wearables, virtual assistants, and more.

We're Putting Our Brains Together

It is unlikely that it will be able to control or drive the underlying Metaverse. True, it is home to the world's second-largest computer platform (and by far the most valuable), as well as the world's largest video game retailers (which also means it pays developers more than anyone else on the planet). Furthermore, the company is heavily investing in augmented reality devices and "connective tissue" that will aid the Metaverse (for example, beacons, Apple Watch, and Apple AirPods). However, Apple's attitude and business model are incompatible with creating an open platform for innovation where anyone can access the full range of user data and device APIs. Apple is more likely to be the primary mode of communication between the Western world and the Metaverse than the operator/driver. Like the Internet, everyone will almost certainly benefit from this.

Unity will be important if the Metaverse requires a wide range of assets, experiences, and shared APIs.

More than half of mobile games use this engine.

In real-world rendering/simulation use cases (architecture, design, and engineering), it is even more popular than Unreal. For example, filmmaker Jon Favreau was producing and filming the photorealistic Lion King in Unity while also producing and filming Disney's The Mandalorian in

35

Unreal. It also runs one of the world's largest digital ad networks (a nice byproduct of powering 10 billion daily minutes of mobile entertainment).

The role of unity in moving the Metaverse forward, on the other hand, is unknown. There is no store, login system, or true direct-to-consumer experience. The majority of its ancillary services (such as non-engine or advertising) are rarely used. Furthermore, rather than serving as Metaverse gateways, the majority (but not all) Unity-powered games are simply mobile games. Given its unavoidable influence on norms, playtime, and content creation, it's difficult to imagine it not being acquired and merged into a larger technology company with more assets and perks.

Purchasing Unity used to be difficult to justify. Regardless of the company's high value, any potential acquirer must keep Unity completely platform neutral in order to maintain market dominance, developer support, and influence (for example, Google couldn't make Unity exclusive to or best on Android/Chrome without alienating a large number of developers). This implies that converting Unity into a proprietary engine is a bad business decision. The value lost as a result of such a decision, combined with the additional cost of purchasing Unity, will almost certainly render such a move unaffordable. The goal of a Unity, on the other hand, The buyer will be motivated to keep the engine open and available across platforms if the acquisition is to gain a key position on the new Internet, and the price will quickly become irrelevant.

If Epic does this, Valve must have a viable way to access the Metaverse. In terms of users, money, and playtime, Valve's

Steam dominates the Epic Games Store. Furthermore, it owns a number of the most popular and long-running multiplayer games on the market (Counter-Strike, Team Fortress, DotA). Furthermore, the company has a long history of content and monetization innovation (it was the first to experiment at scale with AAA free-to-play games and player-to-player marketplaces). Valve has also spent years developing and deploying virtual reality technology, is privately owned by a group of passionate programmers who love open-source technologies and despise closed environments, and generates billions of dollars in annual revenue. In contrast, Valve's Source engine has received little attention. Unlike Epic, it appears to be less concerned with integrating its capabilities and assets in order to develop the Metaverse.

Why Are Holograms Important in the Metaverse?

When the internet was first introduced, it was accompanied by a slew of technological achievements, such as the ability to connect computers over long distances and to link one web page to another.

These technical characteristics laid the groundwork for the abstract structures we now associate with the internet, such as webpages, apps, social networks, and everything else that is built on them. That's not even taking into account the convergence of non-internet interface innovations like displays, keyboards, mice, and touchscreens, which are still required to make the internet work.

There are some new building blocks in place with the metaverse, such as the ability to host hundreds of people in a single instance of a server (future versions of a metaverse should be able to handle thousands, if not millions), and motion-tracking tools that can distinguish where a person's hands are. These new technologies have the potential to be very interesting and futuristic.

There are, however, some constraints that may prove impossible to overcome. Companies such as Microsoft and Fa—Meta display fictitious videos of future concepts, but they frequently gloss over how people will interact with the metaverse. VR headsets are still awkward, and most people get motion sickness or physical pain from wearing them for long periods of time. Aside from the significant challenge of figuring out how to wear augmented reality glasses in public without looking like huge dorks, augmented reality glasses have another issue.

So, how do IT firms demonstrate the concept of their technology without displaying the reality of massive equipment and odd glasses? So far, it appears that their primary option is to build technology from the ground up. Is this the same woman who appeared during Meta's speech? I'm sorry to break the news, but even with the most advanced versions of existing technology, it's simply not possible.

Unlike motion-tracked digital avatars, which are currently a little janky but could be improved tomorrow, there is no janky way of making a three-dimensional image appear in midair without precisely regulated circumstances.

Regardless of Iron Man's claims. Perhaps these are intended to be viewed as images projected through glasses—after all, both women in the demo video are wearing glasses—but that assumes a lot about the physical capabilities of small glasses, which Snap can attest to being a difficult challenge to solve.

This type of reality deception is common in film demonstrations of how the metaverse might work. Is this person wearing virtual reality goggles or is he or she simply sitting at a desk? Is this person attached to an immersive aerial rig, or is he or she simply sitting at a desk? Another of Meta's demos showed people hovering in space—is this person attached to an immersive aerial rig or simply sitting at a desk? Is the subject of the hologram wearing a headset, and if so, how is their face scanned? A person may take virtual objects but appear to hold them in their actual hands at other times.

This protest raises far more questions than it answers.

This is acceptable on some levels. Instead of addressing every technological challenge, Microsoft, Meta, and every other company that creates bizarre demos like this are attempting to convey an artistic sense of what the future might be like. It's a long-standing tradition that dates back to AT&T's demonstration of a voice-controlled folding phone capable of erasing people from photos and creating 3D models, all of which seemed impossible at the time.

On the other hand, this type of wishful-thinking-as-techdemo puts us in a position where it's difficult to predict which aspects of various metaverse ideas will one day become reality. For example, if virtual reality and augmented reality headsets become comfortable and affordable enough for people to wear on a daily basis—a big "if"—the idea of a virtual poker game where your friends are robots and holograms floating in space could become a reality. If not, you could always use a Discord video conference to play Tabletop Simulator.

The glitz and glam of VR and AR also obscures the more mundane aspects of the metaverse, which are more likely to manifest. For example, it would be trivially easy for software companies to develop an open digital avatar standard, which is a type of file that contains features you would enter into a character creator—such as eye colour, hairstyle, or wardrobe options—and allows you to carry it with you wherever you go. There's no reason to create a more comfortable VR headset for that.

CHAPTER 2

UNDERSTANDING AUGMENTED REALITY AND HOW IT WORKS.

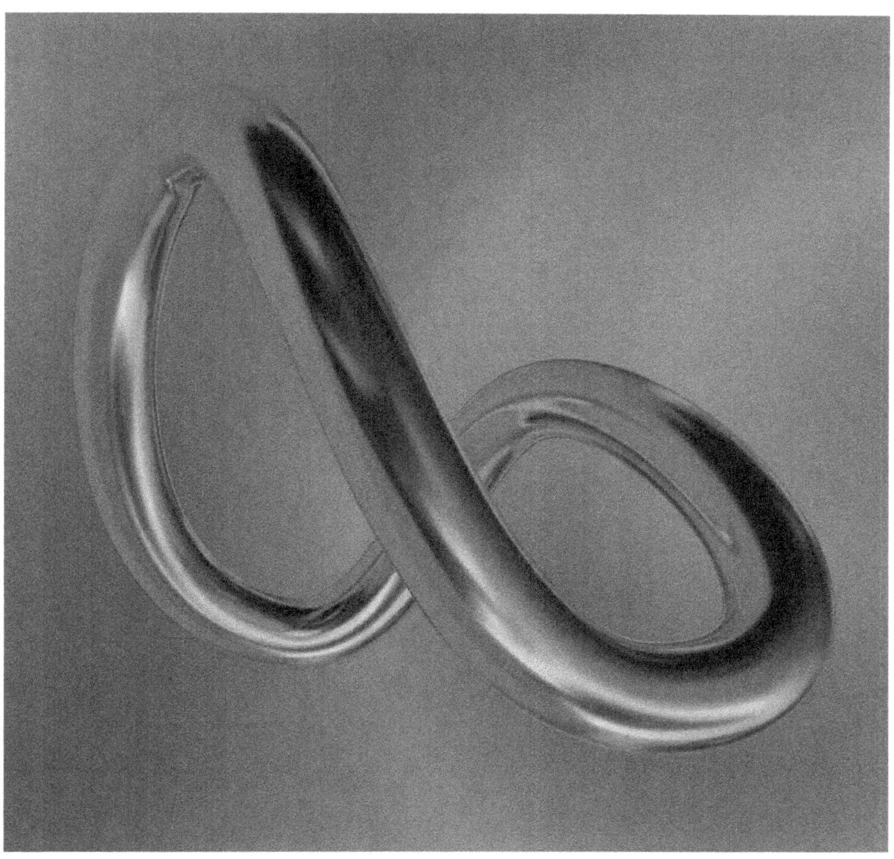

Today's lives are computer-mediated and technologically enhanced. People want more than just to exist in the physical world; they want the richer experiences that technological advancement enables them to have. One of these breakthroughs is augmented reality (AR), a technology that allows people to dance with celebrities, travel to exotic locations, visit other planets, and even travel back in time – all from the comfort of their own homes. Continue reading to learn more about augmented reality and how it works if you want to embrace technological change.

What exactly is Augmented Reality, and how does it function?

So, exactly what is augmented reality? It's difficult to define "augmented reality" because the human experience is fundamentally different from the technical concept it represents. However, in its broadest sense, augmented reality (AR) technology can be defined as a view of a physical environment enhanced by computer-generated visual and/or audio features.

AR's Brief History

In 1901, the same year that L. When Frank Baum's novel "The Master Key" was published, the first hints of augmented reality appeared. Despite the fact that the protagonist's glasses were not named AR, the devil granted him glasses that allowed him to see the letters on people's foreheads that indicated their nature (e.g., E for evil, G for good, W for wisdom, and so on). The "Video Place" AR lab was founded in 1974. Tom Caudell and David Mizell, on the other hand, were the first to document the augmented reality features in 1990.

Julie Martin unveiled the first fully functional augmented reality device in 1994. It was called "Dancing in Cyberspace" for a reason: it was an augmented reality theatre that blended virtual objects with real-world settings.

In the twenty-first century, augmented reality has advanced rapidly. Hirokazu Kato, for example, launched ARToolKit, an opensource AR library, in 2000. It was an innovative use of virtual graphics and real-time video tracking for overlapping images. Nine years later, ARToolkit was seamlessly integrated into web browsers. Google debuted the "Google Glass" project in 2013, and the augmented reality game "Pokemon GO" dominated the world in 2016. The introduction of eye-tracking augmented reality technology in 2017 was a watershed moment. Over 1,000 apps with augmented reality capabilities have been released on the Google and Apple app stores since 2018.

What Is the Distinction Between Augmented and Virtual Reality?

Virtual reality (VR), a technology that immerses the user in a simulated environment while disconnecting him or her from the real world, is frequently confused with augmented reality. The difference between AR and VR is that the former augments reality while the latter replaces it. To supplement the real-time environment, AR proposes the overlaying of digital, computer-generated information (e.g., video, sound, or animation) over it.

Consider a variety of VR and AR devices to gain a better understanding of augmented reality technology.

Among the AR apps are:

• Customers can use Ikea's augmented reality app to locate the right product for their space. They can use their smartphone's camera to look around the room. By swiping and clicking, they can instantly see if a piece of Ikea furniture matches the design in their apartment.

The Gap recently debuted augmented reality-enhanced changing rooms, allowing customers to try on a variety of items without having to lug their belongings across the store.

• Bayern Monaco has launched an augmented reality app that allows fans to take photos with their heroes without having to travel to Munich.

• Drivers can see the engine through the transparent bonnet thanks to Land Rover's augmented reality software.

• Marriott's virtual reality "Transporters" software allows guests to tour the company's properties around the world. The software is realistic and could provide a realistic travel experience.

• SportX's virtual reality simulator allows customers to try on the sportswear they sell while participating in a variety of simulated activities such as jogging, swimming, and tennis.

• The HoloTeach VR app allows surgeons to engage and consult in real-time during an operation, even if they are thousands of miles apart.

AR is an interactive reality that incorporates computer-generated components into the real world, such as video, sound, or graphics/animation, to provide a more immersive experience for the user.

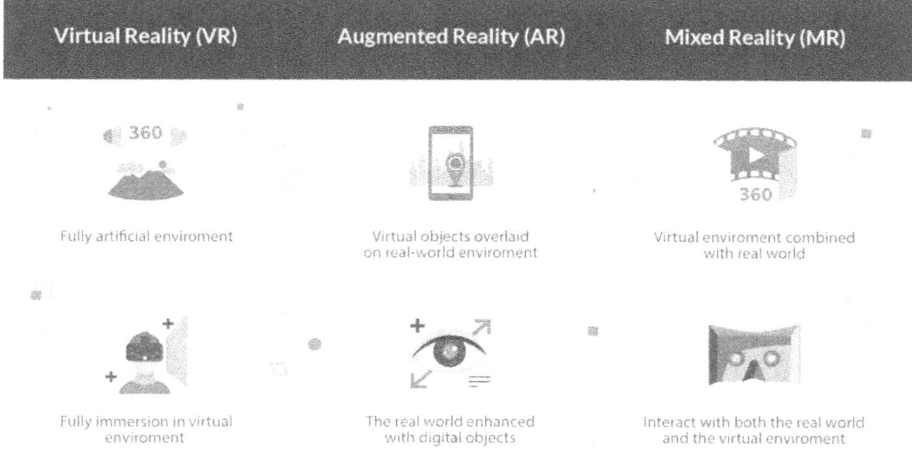

TYPES OF AUGMENTED REALITY

Modern augmented technology comes in a variety of forms as a result of recent breakthroughs in the IT industry. Here's a quick rundown of the most common types of augmented reality that businesses and consumers are using today.

Markers for augmented reality

At the start of AR development, a marker (a thick black square border) was used as a reference item to measure the distance between a computer and the object.

In other words, a marker-based AR app relies on the reader (typically a camera) to interpret an image and generate 3D objects in the virtual environment.

AR without markers

Despite the obvious advantages of marker-based AR, the thick black marker's visual appearance was unappealing, limiting market adoption of market-based solutions.

The markerless AR was developed primarily for business use in order to address the shortcomings of the previous generation.

In this AR type, general images are used as markers, which are provided by image extraction techniques such as SIFT, SURF, and FAST-SURF. To address the issue of robustness caused by outliers, massive occlusion, and other factors, the most recent markerless AR systems employ the robust point matching approach. It can detect and map the real-world environment and place virtual items within it. Markerless AR can be anything from a dancing animated creature on the table to an IKEA sofa placed in your home.

AR-based on projection

As the name implies, the projection-based version of AR employs a video projector to display images on a screen or a variety of physical surfaces. The use of real-world objects for the projection of virtual images is central to this AR category. It's commonly used for product visualisation and industrial assembly. However, portable projection-based Because of reflectance, colour, and geometry variations, AR projection quality is limited to a degree on diverse, oddly shaped surfaces.

AR-based on superimposition

This type of augmented reality assumes that graphical changes to the real thing are superimposed directly on it (or its fully replicated image), resulting in an augmented view of the real thing. Because the inability of technology to recognize objects prevents the original image from being replaced with an augmented view, the ability of technology to recognize things is important in superimposition-based AR execution. A good example of this type of augmented reality is the real-time medical evaluation of patients. Some medical facilities, for example, provide a live feed from X-ray equipment, allowing the X-ray results to be superimposed on an image of the patient's body.

WHERE DOES AUGMENTED REALITY COME FROM AND HOW DOES IT WORK?

AR applications are no longer just for fun.

This technology has numerous business, scientific, and research applications. Here are some details about the processes and tools used to create immersive augmented reality experiences.

Sensors and cameras

Any AR element requires the exact capture of real-world items in order to realistically augment them on your display. For these purposes, the AR programme employs a variety of sensors, including mechanical, biological, acoustic, optical, and environmental sensors.

Mechanical sensors record the position, shape, acceleration, mass, and displacement of an object. One of the most common applications is determining the position, weight, and movements of an object.

Biological sensors measure the object's heart rate, temperature, neural activity, and respiration rate. They are capable of detecting moods and assessing people's mental and physical states.

Acoustic sensors provide accurate sound loudness, pitch, frequency, phase, and modulation information, which is extremely useful for sound detection and speech recognition.

Optical sensors report an object's emissivity, refraction, lightwave frequency, brightness, and luminance, which is useful for computer vision detection, presence detection, and IR motion analysis.

Environmental sensors collect data on the temperature and humidity of the surrounding environment.

One of the most important tools for creating engaging AR experiences is the depth-sensing camera, which can collect 3D images. AR devices have traditionally had at least one camera, with some having two for depth sensing. It's also common for the device to include an infrared camera for advanced depth-sensing and heat mapping.

Projection

Projection is an augmented reality technology that allows users to augment real-world objects without the need for wearable or portable devices. It means that augmented reality features are displayed directly on objects using spatial AR tools using programmable projector-camera systems.

Projection AR systems are cutting-edge augmented reality technologies because they offer completely unrestricted

AR experiences, allowing users to enjoy projection on the go by projecting augmented reality features onto the environment.

The ability to process AR is primarily due to advanced image and sound processing techniques. Image processing is used in all AR products to accurately understand the environment, estimate light, and determine essential feature points and planes.

Reflection

AR technology's primary purpose is to create photorealistic visuals by integrating virtual items into real-world surroundings. When a developer uses advanced modelling to integrate virtual and actual environments, he or she can create realistic visuals. Virtual reflection, for example, is an augmented reality technology that simulates real-world object reflections on virtual objects, enhancing real-life scenarios.

WHAT KINDS OF DEVICES DOES AUGMENTED REALITY SUPPORT?

After you've mastered the fundamentals of augmented reality, you might want to learn more about the devices that make it possible.

Cell Phones

Though a few decades ago, AR could only be experienced in properly equipped rooms with a lot of specialist technology, today's smartphone apps provide realistic AR experiences. Both iOS and Android devices now support augmented reality. Popular apps include the world-famous game Pokemon Go, as well as BBC Civilizations AR, Froggipedia, and SketchAR. Popular messengers and social media platforms also allow us to experiment with the potential of augmented reality (e.g., Hololens, Snapchat filters, etc.).

AR-Enabled Devices

While mobile technology is rapidly evolving, bringing new inventions to the world, more realistic, advanced, and professional-looking augmented reality (AR) is still only available through the use of specialized AR devices such as wearable smart glasses, head-mounted apparatuses, digital compasses, gyroscopes, CPUs, GPSs, and displays. The most common special gadget is the head-up display (HUD), which a user wears to get a completely immersive AR experience.

Augmented Reality Glasses

Smart glasses have grown in popularity as well, with companies such as Google Glasses and Laster SeeThru gaining a lot of traction. AR-enhanced lenses have also been incorporated into lightweight AR spectacles, such as the AV Walker, which overlays the real world with digital content.

Contact Lenses with Augmented Reality

The incorporation of augmented reality technology into contact lenses is a relatively new trend in the world of technology.

The University of Washington has launched a ground-breaking project called "Twinkle in the Eye" to create AR lenses that can display texts, translate speech into captions, and deliver visual cues from the navigation system in real time.

Virtual Retina Display (VRD) (VRD)

VRD was introduced as cutting-edge technology for creating visual images in the late 1990s.

The first one was created by the Human Interface Technology Laboratory (HIT Lab). The VRD's image synthesis process is based on low-power laser light scanning and direct image reproduction on the human retina. As a result, the VRD allows for the creation of high-resolution, high-contrast visuals that can be superimposed over whatever the user sees.

What are the Augmented Reality Controls?

Developers have currently created features and functionalities that can govern the functionality of AR apps.

The user, for example, decides how to act, which scenario to follow, and when the game should end.

In contrast, new AR apps are expected to be controlled by the human mind. Though it may be difficult to imagine now, such power is unquestionably attainable in the coming years. Startups such as Neurable are taking the first steps toward allowing users to navigate VR and AR apps with a "brain mouse."

The Future Importance of Augmented Reality

As technology advances at an unprecedented rate, we can expect AR to advance quickly, bringing brand-new experiences to users all over the world. So, what is the future of those who use augmented reality?

• Augmented reality contact lenses While AR lens prototypes are already in use, widespread adoption is still a long way off. Wireless lenses with hundreds of LEDs forming images in front of the human eye, on the other hand, are expected to be available soon. These visuals may include words, charts, photographs, active instructions, and fun AR components. • Bionic Eyes are a set of bionic eyes. As biomimicry and bionics evolve rapidly, humanity can expect the introduction of AR technology in this sector.

Bionic eyes, for example, could help the blind or those with poor vision restore their vision.

As you can see, augmented reality is a promising field of technology that has the potential to improve visual experiences while also changing how people learn, navigate, receive medical treatment, and communicate. AR devices are becoming more sophisticated, user-friendly, and lightweight, bringing AR experiences to everyday consumers and allowing them to have fun, learn new things, travel to faraway places, and meet people from all over the world in a single room.

CHAPTER 3

NFT'S ROLE IN THE METAVERSE

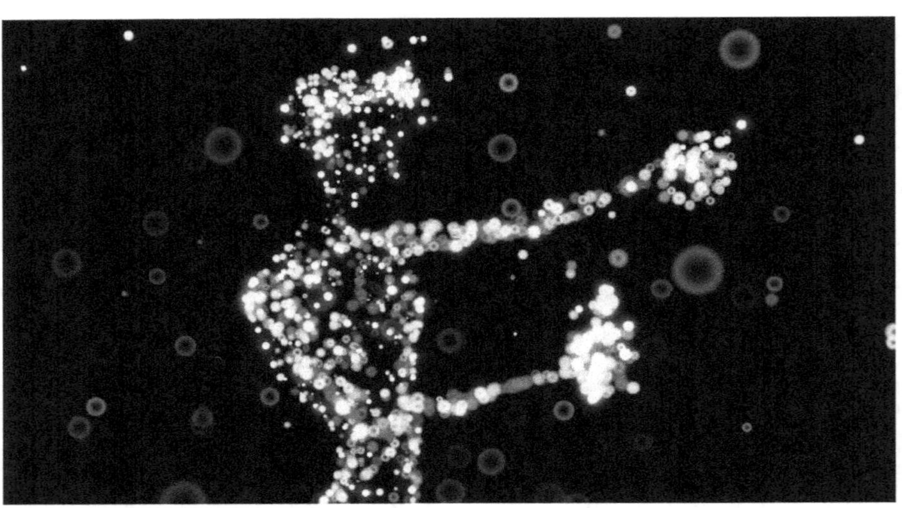

With their rapidly expanding use cases, NFTs are ushering in a new era of the digital world known as the Metaverse.

The launch of Meta by Facebook, signalling the transition to a metaverse era in which NFT-based augmented experiences are likely to serve as pillars for next-generation social networks, best exemplifies the arrival of metaverses on the global stage.

NFTs and metaverses are already inextricably linked, most notably in blockchain gaming and other interoperable games, where they serve as value carriers for large-scale digital social media. Despite being a relatively new concept, NFT gaming is popular, as evidenced by Binance NFT's Initial Game Offering (IGO). This new gaming arm has received such positive feedback from gamers and cryptocurrency consumers that it has already surpassed $16 million in trade volume in just two weeks, with all of IGO's NFT collections sold out.

What Exactly Is the Metaverse, and How Does It Work?

A metaverse is a blockchain-powered digital ecosystem. Technologies such as VR and AR provide visual components, while decentralized media allows for limitless social engagement and business opportunities. These environments are scalable, interoperable, and adaptable, combining novel technology and interaction models among members on both an individual and organisational level.

Metaverses are digital 3D universes that include communications, money, gaming worlds, personal profiles, NFTs, and other processes and elements. The promise metaverse's is attributed to the freedom it provides; anyone in the metaverse can build, buy, and view NFTs to amass virtual land, join social communities, construct virtual identities, and play games, among other things. With enterprises and individuals alike able to integrate into metaverse frameworks, this diverse range of use cases opens up many possibilities for monetizing real-world and digital assets.

Future metaverses will bring disparate online worlds together, with NFTs enabling cross-chain interactions. Read on to learn more about the metaverse.

WHAT WILL THE IMPACT OF NFTS BE ON THE METAVERSE?

In the metaverse, NFTs have the potential to disrupt the traditional social network paradigm of user contact, socialisation, and transaction.

Discover how NFTs can wreak havoc in the digital world.

An Economic System That Is Both Open And Fair

Users and businesses can now move physical assets and services to the metaverse, a decentralized virtual environment. One method for bringing more real-world assets into the metaverse is to use novel gaming models with interoperable blockchain games.

The play-to-earn gaming concept, for example, engages and empowers blockchain game players.

Players can participate in the metaverse's in-game economies and earn incentives for the value they provide by relying on NFTs, essentially earning while they play. Play-to-earn games are also fair in the metaverse because participants retain complete ownership of their assets rather than a single game entity, as in most traditional games.

Assume you want to participate in these in-game financial economies. In that case, Binance NFT's IGO launches offer a variety of in-game assets from gaming projects that players can collect and integrate into various gaming environments. Such in-game NFTs are extremely popular, as evidenced by IGO debuts, where all NFTs were sold out on the first day. Successful play-to-earn games include My Neighbor Alice (Alice), Axie Infinite (AXS), and many others.

Play-to-earn gaming guilds will also help to increase the popularity of play-to-earn gaming. Guilds act as intermediaries by purchasing in-game NFT resources such as land and assets and then lending them out to players looking to make money in their virtual worlds. The earnings are then distributed among the play-to-earn guilds.

This promotes an open and fair economy by giving players who do not have the necessary funds to join guilds a head start. Furthermore, guilds lower the entry barrier to play-to-earn games for all players, ensuring that everyone has an equal opportunity to participate in the metaverse economy. In summary, guilds aid in the establishment of virtual economies in the metaverse by making NFT resources more accessible to all.

One such example is Yield Guild Games (YGG). They establish a global community of metaverse participants who contribute to virtual worlds in exchange for in-world rewards and earn money by renting or selling YGG-owned assets for a profit. In-world assets can command real-world value because users can exchange their NFT assets, such as in-game assets and digital real estate, on NFT platforms like Binance NFT. The economic value of the NFTs available in-game is determined by their use in various metaverse modules. This enables users to create any type of content they want, such as popular assets that appeal to a wide audience, original digital artwork, or specialised NFTs that confer specific skills and appearances in games.

Metaverses enable an open and fair economy, aided by the blockchain's immutability and transparency. Furthermore, prices are determined by the fundamental law of supply and demand, which is based on scarcity and the on-chain value of an NFT based on its applicability, eliminating the possibility of pumps and artificial value inflation.

NFT's game drops are an example of Binance's aided way of operating the metaverse economy.

Weekly IGO releases provide key in-game assets from gaming projects, allowing players to get a head start in the NFT gaming industry. In addition, one-of-a-kind Mystery Boxes with various valuable items for play-to-win games will drop.

Users can find and trade in-game NFT items on the Binance NFT secondary marketplace. Binance NFT also curates a daily set of suggestions for NFT collections and creators on the homepage and ranking boards to promote the top NFT sales, collections, and producers to help NFT newcomers.

Experiences of Identity, Community, and Sociality Expanded NFTs will also play an important role in metaverse identity, community, and social interactions. For example, holding specific NFT assets can communicate a user's support for a project or thoughts on the virtual and real worlds. This enables people with similar NFTs to form communities, share their experiences, and collaborate on content creation. Trending NFT avatars are one type of NFT.

The NFT avatar represents a player's true or imagined self. NFT avatars can be used as access tokens to enter and move around the metaverse.

59

In this situation, NFT avatars serve as an extension of our real-life identities, allowing us to curate and create our virtual identities in the metaverse with complete control and independence.

Avatar NFTs enable virtual membership in a variety of unique metaverse and physical world activities, fostering community and social interactions. NFT avatars are already shaping the experiences and environments of the metaverses through content creation and company launches.

The Bored Ape Yacht Club and CryptoPunks collections, for example, give their holders exclusive rights and access to gated groups of affluent people with protected content, as well as offline exclusive events. Furthermore, exclusive parties with NFT-related entrance fees highlight the function of NFTs as value carriers that connect the digital and physical worlds.

To find and purchase NFT avatars, visit the Binance NFT Marketplace, which has a large selection of low-cost NFT avatar options.

Property Ownership in Virtual Real Estate

With NFTs, users can have complete control over their virtual lands and spaces in the metaverse. Furthermore, thanks to the underlying blockchain, users can prove ownership of the item and build their virtual real estate as they see fit.

Selling a property for profit, renting land for passive income, creating various structures such as online shops on existing land, and hosting social gatherings are some of the uses for virtual real estate in the metaverse.

Decentraland is an example of the metaverse's digital real estate scene, having recently organised a virtual fashion exhibition with Adidas, where creations were auctioned off as NFTs. Musicians are particularly interested in virtual real estate because it allows them to perform and sell NFT tickets and products online.

While still in their infancy, metaverses offer a plethora of potential social and financial opportunities through the use of NFTs, as well as new ways for people to play, engage, congregate, earn, and transact.

Metaverses and NFT blockchain gaming will be an important part of Web 3.0, a period in which real-world businesses expand into the digital domain and users discover the adaptability of such settings by incorporating VR, video games, social networking, and elements of crypto.

We believe that NFT ownership is critical and will open up a world of possibilities in the coming metaverses. Users who want to explore the metaverse can use the Binance NFT Marketplace to find, accumulate, and exchange one-of-a-kind NFT assets.

CHAPTER 4

THE WEB 3.0

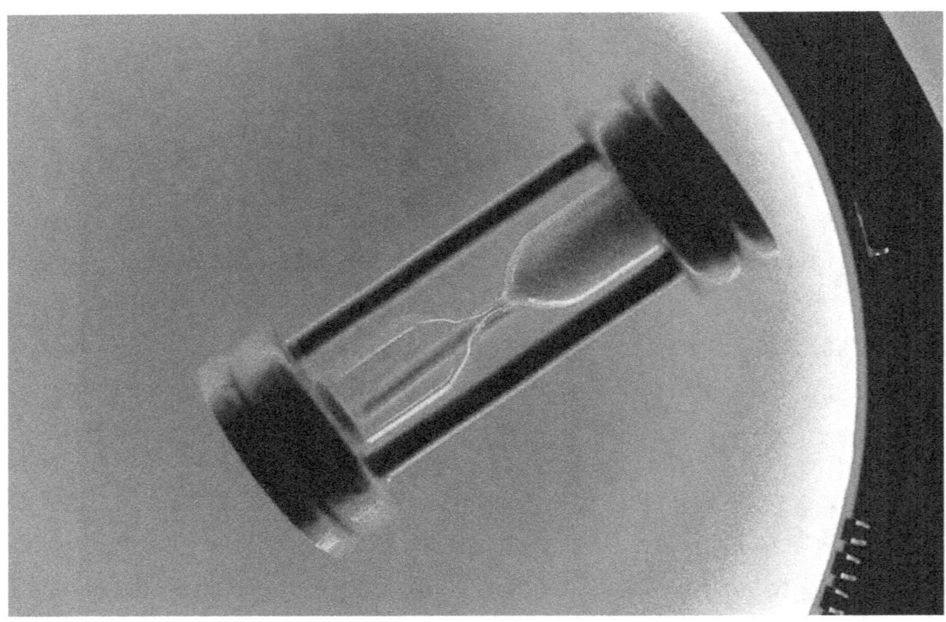

You may have come across the term "Web3" if you've been reading cryptocurrency forums or videogame news recently—or seeing everything from New York Times job listings to zany Twitter threads claiming that the traditional job interview is about to be replaced by blockchain-based "quests, adventures, and courses to prove your worth." The name alludes to the third generation of the internet. Is it, however, just jargon among those who trade NFTs of cartoon apes for hundreds of thousands of dollars and are already planning their metaverse mansions? Shouldn't those who thought we were still on Web2 be aware of Web3 and the less focused form of the internet it represents? Both of these questions will almost certainly be answered in the affirmative. The answers to your follow-up questions are provided below.

What exactly is Web3?

Web3 is a potential future internet version based on public blockchains, a record-keeping system best known for facilitating cryptocurrency transactions. Web3 is appealing because it is decentralized, which means that rather than consumers accessing the internet through services mediated by companies such as Google, Apple, or Facebook, individuals own and govern sections of the internet themselves. Furthermore, web3 does not require "permission," which means that central authorities do not have the authority to decide who has access to what services, nor does it require "trust," which means that an intermediary is not required to allow virtual transactions between two or more parties. Finally, because these agencies and intermediaries collect the majority of the data, Web3 technically protects user privacy more effectively.

Of course, while this is a utopian vision of Web3 for the future envisioned by blockchain engineers and supporters, it may not be as equitable in practice. For example, decentralized finance, also known as DeFi, is a growing component of Web3. It entails carrying out real-world financial transactions on the blockchain without the assistance of banks or governments.

63

Meanwhile, many major corporations and venture capital firms are pouring money into Web3, and it's difficult to imagine that their participation will not result in some form of centralised power.

What was Web3's forerunner?

Web1 and Web2 (also known as Web 2.0) are terms used to refer to earlier internet eras. Web1 refers to the period between the 1990s and the early 2000s when the internet was more decentralized and open-source protocols were more popular. Static pages, or websites that cannot be interacted with and are not updated on a regular basis, were more common. Web2 refers to the period from the early 2000s to the present in which Big Tech companies control the most important online hubs. Another sign of this era is the proliferation of user-generated content on galaxy-sized platforms, such as YouTube videos or Facebook posts. This is the stuff that keeps social media running. Instead of being a place for passive consumption, the internet has evolved into a place for active participation.

But wait, isn't Web3 a cryptocurrency?

Web3 will make extensive use of NFTs, digital currencies, and other blockchain entities. Reddit, for example, hopes to break into the Web3 space by developing a method that uses cryptocurrency tokens to give users control over portions of the communities they participate in on the site.

Users would earn "community points" by posting on a specific subreddit, according to the idea. The user is then rewarded with points based on how many people upvote or downvote a specific post. (It's essentially a blockchain-based version of Reddit Karma.) Those points can essentially be used as voting shares, allowing users who have made significant contributions to have a greater say in community decisions. Furthermore, because those points are stored on the blockchain, their owners have greater control over them; they cannot be easily taken away, and you can be tracked. To be fair, this is just one application, a corporate interpretation of the Web3 concept of Decentralized Autonomous Organizations, or DAOs, which use tokens to divide ownership and decision-making authority. Augur, a decentralized betting platform, is an example of a decentralized autonomous organisation (DAO). NFTs play an important role in Web3.

They're basically one-of-a-kind cryptocurrency tokens that are commonly used as certificates of ownership for virtual items like artwork or basketball footage. (As opposed to a Bitcoin, which can be exchanged for any other Bitcoin.) According to Web3 supporters, the digital scarcity represented by NFTs will allow users of this new internet to exchange anything from video game skins to medical records.

Why is there suddenly so much interest in Web3?

Much of the excitement appears to be coming from the bitcoin community, which stands to benefit from a more reliant internet on its technology. Some of the buzzes, however, stem from a few well-known companies, such as Reddit, taking proactive steps to establish Web3 services and platforms ahead of the curve. According to CoinDesk, GameStop is looking for a "Head of Web3 Gaming" and software engineers for an unidentified NFT platform. Furthermore, there has been a lot of discussion about how Web3 could improve video games by making it easier for players to buy and trade in-game items or earn tokens that give them more control over how the game is governed. The Verge speculated, however, that GameStop may simply be using terms like "Web3" and "blockchain" in its job postings to attract the same kind of alternative investor support it received in January. A more recent development was the venture capital firm Andreessen Horowitz's Web3 lobbying push in Washington, D.C., in early October. According to the company, Web3, which has heavily invested in bitcoin and other blockchain technology, has sent executives to Capitol Hill and the White House to promote Web3 as a solution to Silicon Valley consolidation and to propose rules for the expanding virtual world.

Isn't the hype surrounding Web3 entirely reasonable and measured?

Late in October, a 28-year-old artist shared the meme "Love in the Time of Web3," which depicted a cartoon couple lying in bed and staring at Bitcoin and Ethereum prices. After billionaire Elon Musk tweeted it and received hundreds of thousands of likes, the artist was able to turn the meme into an NFT and sell it for nearly $20,000 dollars. In other news, a group that aspires to be a "Web3 streetwear band" produces NFTs with cartoon apes attached. At a recent auction, one of the cartoon monkeys fetched $3.4 million. So, in response to the question, the answer is no. What is Web3's role in the metaverse?

IT IS VERY POPULAR IN TECHNOLOGY.

66

I mentioned that our hosts had not been vaccinated. As a result, my Airbnb review has been deleted.

Why Are Astronomers "crying and puking all over"? Because of the upcoming launch of a telescope

Every Baby Boomer's Red Eye Was Caused by an Obsolete Object

The Controversial Plan to Remove Carbon from the Atmosphere

To begin, the metaverse is a futuristic internet comprised of three-dimensional virtual reality areas where users can interact with one another. Because of this, Facebook recently renamed itself "Meta." According to some technologists, Web3 will spur the development of a metaverse based on blockchain technology and open standards, managed by a global network of computers rather than a few large corporations. Traditional gatekeepers would be unable to control what could and could not enter the metaverse if NFTs were used to allow virtual reality trade. In an October public statement, Facebook CEO Mark Zuckerberg waxed poetic about how the metaverse will not "be produced by one firm" and will establish "a significantly broader creative economy than that confined by today's platforms and policies." All of this sounds wonderful, but given how hard Facebook has fought to maintain its dominance in the social media scene, it appears likely that it will continue to try to maintain its prominence even in the Web3 future.

WHICH NEW BUSINESS MODELS WILL BE AVAILABLE AS A RESULT OF WEB 3.0?

Web 3.0 will have far-reaching consequences that extend well beyond cryptocurrency's initial use case. Because of the richness of interactions now possible and the global scope of counterparties available, Web 3.0 will cryptographically connect data from corporations, people, and machines with efficient machine learning techniques, resulting in the emergence of fundamentally new markets and associated business models.

The future impact of Web 3.0 is clear, but the question remains as to which business models can break the code and create long-term and sustainable value in today's economy.

A look back at business models from the 1.0, 2.0, and 3.0 eras of the Internet.

After briefly touching on the oft-forgotten but often arduous journeys that led to Web 2.0's surprising and unpredictable successful business models, we'll dive into the native business models that Web 3.0 has enabled and will enable.

Let us not forget Google's journey from 1998 to 2002 before going public in 2004 in order to lay the groundwork for Web 2.0's business model discovery process:

• Despite having a high volume of traffic, they clearly suffered from a poor business plan in 1999. "We really couldn't figure out the business strategy; there was a time when things looked bleak," said Mike Moritz (Sequoia Capital), their lead investor.

• Google made $85 million in revenue in 2001, while Overture made $288 million, as CPM-based web advertising faded following the dot-com crash.

• Based on Overture's ad strategy, Google launched AdWords Select in 2002, its own pay-per-click, auction-based search-advertising product.

• Two years later, in 2004, Google accounted for 84.7 percent of all internet searches and went public, valued at $23.2 billion and generating $2.7 billion in annualised revenue.

After four years of struggle, a single small change in their business plan launched Google into orbit, propelling it to become one of the world's most valuable companies.

Looking back at the Web 2.0 Business Models Content

The first forms of online content were simply digitizations of existing newspapers and telephone directories...

Regardless, Roma (Alfonso Cuarón) has received ten Academy Award nominations for a film distributed via Netflix's subscription streaming service.

Marketplaces

Amazon began as an online bookstore that no one anticipated would be profitable... Regardless, it has grown into a massive marketplace selling everything from gardening tools to healthy foods to cloud infrastructure.

Software that is open-source and free

Open-source software development began as a hobby and a utopian vision of software as a publicly available common

69

good... Regardless, the entire internet now runs on open-source software, generating $400 billion in economic value per year, and Github was purchased by Microsoft for $7.5 billion. In comparison, Red Hat earns $3.4 billion per year from Linux services.

SaaS It may have seemed impossible in the early days of Web 2.0 that business software could be delivered via browser and be economically viable... Despite this, most B2B organisations now use SaaS models.

The Sharing Economy

It was difficult to imagine anyone willingly getting into someone else's car or lending their couch to strangers...

Despite not owning any cars or houses, Uber and AirBnB have grown to become the world's largest taxi and lodging companies.

While Google and Facebook experienced rapid growth in their early years, they lacked a clear income strategy for the first half of their existence... Nonetheless, the advertising model seemed almost too well suited to them. As a result, they now account for 58% of global digital advertising revenues ($111 billion in 2018), making them the dominant Web 2.0 economic model.

Web 3.0 Business Models are Taking Off

If you examine Web 3.0 over the last ten years, you'll notice that the early business models aren't always repeatable or scalable, and they frequently attempt to recreate Web 2.0

concepts. While there is some doubt about their viability, we are confident that continued experimentation by some of the most skilled builders will result in extremely valuable models in the coming years.

By investigating both existing and experimental Web 3.0 business models, we hope to learn how some of the more established and experimental Web 3.0 business models will accumulate value in the coming years.

• The creation of a native asset • The maintenance of the native asset and the expansion of the network:

• Speculation-related taxes (exchanges) • Payment tokens

• Tokens should be burned • Work tokens • Additional models

The following steps are involved in the issuance of a native asset:

The first cryptocurrency was Bitcoin. Proof of Work and Nakamoto Consensus were used to create the first Byzantine Fault Tolerant and fully open peer-to-peer network. Its core business model is based on BTC, a digital coin that is provably scarce and distributed to miners as block rewards. Others have followed suit, with the issuance of ETH, XMR, and ZEC by Ethereum, Monero, and ZCash, respectively.

The value of these indigenous assets is derived from the security they provide: By providing a sufficient incentive for honest miners to provide hashing power, the cost for malicious actors to carry out an attack rises in lockstep with the price of the native asset, and the increased security drives further demand for the currency, driving up its price and value. The worth of these indigenous assets has been thoroughly investigated and quantified.

Keeping the indigenous asset while expanding the network:

Some of the first crypto network companies set out with a single goal in mind: to make their networks more profitable and lucrative. The resulting business model can be summarised as "grow their native asset treasury; build the ecosystem." Blockstream, for example, relies on its BTC balance sheet to generate value as one of the largest Bitcoin Core maintainers. Similarly, ConsenSys has grown to a thousand employees in order to increase the value of the ETH it holds by building critical infrastructure for the Ethereum ecosystem.

While this effectively connects firms to networks, the approach is difficult to replicate after the first few companies: amassing a significant enough balance of local assets becomes impractical after a while... The blood, toil, tears, and sweat of founding and maintaining a firm cannot be justified without a significant, enough investment for exponential returns. It would be illogical, for example, for any company other than a central bank — such as a US remittance service — to build a business solely on holding massive amounts of USD while working to improve the US economy.

Native Asset Taxation for Speculative Value:

The next generation of business models focused on developing the financial infrastructure for these native assets, such as exchanges, custodians, and derivatives suppliers. They were all designed with the same goal in mind: to provide services to users who wanted to speculate on these risky assets. While companies such as Coinbase, Bitstamp, and Bitmex have grown to be multibillion-dollar enterprises, they are not monopolistic in the sense that they provide convenience and increase the value of their underlying networks. Because the underlying networks are open and permissionless, companies cannot secure a monopolistic position by providing "exclusive access," but their liquidity and branding can provide defensible moats over time.

Tokens of exchange:

With the rise of the token sale, a new wave of blockchain initiatives built their business models around payment tokens within networks, frequently forming two-sided marketplaces and requiring the use of a native token for all payments. According to the assumptions, as the network's economy grows, so will demand the restricted native payment token, causing the token's value to rise. While the value accrual of such a token paradigm is debatable, the additional friction for the customer is undeniable. What was originally paid in ETH or DAI now necessitates additional exchanges on both sides of the transaction. While this paradigm was popular during the 2017 token frenzy, its friction-inducing characteristics have pushed it to the back of the development queue in the last nine months.

Token Burning: Communities, corporations, and initiatives that generate revenue with a token may not always directly pass earnings on to token holders. The concept of token burns / buybacks sparked a lot of interest as one of the features of the Binance (BNB) and MakerDAO (MKR) tokens. Native tokens are purchased from the open market and burned as revenue flows into the project (via Binance trading fees and

MakerDAO stability fees), resulting in a decrease in token supply and an increase in price. It's fascinating to read Arjun Balaji's analysis (The Block). He claims that the Binance token burning mechanism does not truly result in an equity buyback because no dividends are paid out, leaving the "income per token" at $0.

Tokens for Work:

The work token is a concept that focuses entirely on the network's revenue-generating supply side in order to eliminate friction for users. We see 'hold water' as one of the business models for crypto-networks. Two good examples are Augur's REP and Keep Network's KEEP coins.

Work tokens function in the same way that taxi medallions do. They require service providers to stake/bond a certain amount of native tokens in exchange for the right to perform profitable network work. The ability of the work token paradigm to incentivize actors with a carrot and a stick (rewards for labour) is one of its most important properties (a stake that can be slashed). They can also be judged based on predictable future payment flows to the collective of service providers, and they can provide network security by incentivizing service providers to do honest work (because they have locked skin in the game denominated in the labour token). In a nutshell, such tokens should be priced using future predicted cash flows attributed to all network service providers, which can be modelled using network pricing and usage assumptions.

A number of different models are being investigated, and the following are worth mentioning:

• Dual token models, such as MKR/DAI and SPANK/BOOTY, in which one asset absorbs the volatile ups and downs of consumption while keeping the other stable for optimal transactions.

• Governance tokens provide the ability to influence criteria such as fees and development priorities, and they can be valued as a form of fork insurance.

• Tokenised securities are digital representations of existing assets (shares, commodities, bills, or real estate) with the potential for divisibility and borderless liquidity.

Why Transaction fees for features such as the BloXroute and Aztec Protocol models have been experimenting with a treasury that accepts a small transaction fee in exchange for improvements (e.g., scalability and privacy, respectively).

• Tech 4 Tokens, as proposed by the Starkware team, aims to offer its technology as an investment in exchange for tokens, thereby creating a treasury of all the projects on which they collaborate.

• Providing UX/UI for protocols like Veil and Guesser for Augur and Balance for the MakerDAO ecosystem in exchange for small fees, referrals, and commissions.

• Network-specific services, such as staking (e.g., Staked.us), CDP managers (e.g., topping off MakerDAO CDPs before they become undercollateralized), or marketplace administration services (e.g., OB1 on OpenBazaar), for which traditional fees (subscription or as a percentage of revenues) can be charged.

• Providers of liquidity with revenue-generating business models in non-revenue-generating applications.

For example, Uniswap is a fully automated market maker whose sole source of revenue is the provision of liquidity pairs.

With so many new business models emerging and being investigated, it's clear that, while traditional venture capital has its place, the role of the investor and capital itself is changing. The capital transforms into a native asset within the network, serving a specific function.

Investors must reposition themselves for this new organisational mode, which is driven by trust-minimized decentralized networks, shifting from passive network participation to bootstrapping networks after cash commitment (e.g., computational work or liquidity provision) to direct injections of qualitative work into the networks (e.g., governance).

Looking back, we can see that developing the right business models that resulted in today's tech titans took a lot of trial and error during Web 1.0 and Web 2.0. Of course, we're not dismissing the fact that Web 3.0 will require a similar iterative process, but once we find the right business models, they'll be extremely powerful. Individuals and businesses will be able to interact on a whole new level in trust-free environments, without the need for rent-seeking intermediaries.

Thousands of brilliant teams are already working to put some of these ideas into action or to discover entirely new viable business models. Of course, because the models may not fit traditional frameworks, investors may need to adapt by taking on new roles and providing work and capital (a journey we have already started at Fabric Ventures), but as long as we can see predictable and rational value accrual, it makes sense to double down, as the execution risk diminishes by the day.

CHAPTER 5

STOCKS IN THE METAVERSE YOU SHOULD CONSIDER BUYING

In recent months, the metaverse, which is defined as immersive and interactive virtual online environments, has piqued the interest of the investing and business worlds. As a result, businesses of all sizes are investing billions of dollars in an attempt to capitalise on the internet's next big thing. Meta Platforms (NASDAQ: FB) is the parent company of Facebook,

Oculus, Instagram, and WhatsApp. The IT behemoth intends to invest more than $10 billion in the metaverse each year.

However, Meta isn't the only company involved in the metaverse. Here are three metaverse stocks to invest in right now to capitalise on this long-term trend.

1. Group Matches

Match Group dominates the online dating industry (NASDAQ: MTCH). It owns several applications and services, the most well-known of which is Tinder, the world's most popular mobile dating app. The majority of the company's revenue is currently generated through subscription or a la carte sales. They provide users with more services and expose their dating profiles to more potential matches. Match Group's paying users increased 16 percent year on year to 16.3 million in the most recent quarter, implying that 16.3 million people spent money on the company's various services.

This technique has been proven to be effective thus far, and it should continue to be so in the coming years. Match Group, on the other hand, has stated in its most recent shareholder letter its intention to make its services even more immersive over the next decade. This will begin with video capabilities, which Match Group has already integrated into a number of its products. Tinder, for example, has recently launched a "explore" section where users can connect based on shared interests or activities. Furthermore, it intends to launch a global virtual currency to facilitate the purchase of virtual goods and services on the platform.

Outside of Tinder, Match Group's most ambitious project is Single Town in South Korea, which is managed by its most recent acquisition, Hyperconnect. Single Town is an experimental virtual world in which singles can meet, converse, and hang out in a virtual setting using avatars.

Although the concept is novel and unlikely to be adopted, it reflects Match Group's commitment to improving the services it owns.

2. Take-Two Interactive Inc.

Take-Two Interactive (NASDAQ: TTWO) is a video game developer and publisher best known for games like Grand Theft Auto, Red Dead Redemption, and NBA 2K. GTA, its most metaverse-like franchise, is its main source of revenue. To put things in perspective, GTA V, released in 2013, was Take-most Two's most recent premium GTA game. It was one of the most popular games in the previous decade, and it continues to be a major source of revenue for the company.

What gives that this is even a possibility? Take-Two Interactive released GTA Online alongside GTA V. GTA Online is a virtual world set in San Andreas, a fictional Southern California metropolis. Since the launch of GTA Online, Take-Two has consistently released upgrades and expansions for the community, which has increased spending on virtual goods and services. While not as immersive as virtual reality headsets, GTA Online is probably the best example of a living metaverse in operation right now (at least not yet).

To increase the number of people who can interact in the virtual world, GTA Online will be released as a standalone game in March 2022. The final release of GTA VI, whenever it happens, will almost certainly result in even more recurring interaction in the GTA Online universe.

GTA Online will undoubtedly become more immersive in the coming decade as the virtual world becomes more immersive, which will benefit any Take-Two Interactive owners.

3. The game Roblox

Roblox (NYSE: RBLX) is another metaverse stock, but it "flips the script" when compared to Match Group and Take-Two Interactive. Rather than creating its own metaverse-like experiences, Roblox gives other developers the tools they need to create virtual worlds for users.

Consider it the YouTube of virtual worlds and video games.

Because the majority of Roblox's users are under the age of 18, the platform's experiences are primarily geared toward children.

However, the company believes that over time, it will be able to improve its graphics production tools, bringing its games closer to those released by professional studios like Take-Two. Roblox is already a massive online community, with 47.3 million daily active users (DAUs) at the end of the third quarter. These customers are spending their money on Robux, the platform's in-game currency that developers can use to provide in-game experiences or items. (Roblox makes money by taking a percentage of every transaction.)

In the third quarter, Roblox's net bookings (their sales measure) totaled $637.8 million, generating $170.6 million in free cash flow. As previously stated, the platform is now geared toward children, while Roblox is developing one of the world's most pure-play metaverse systems. As a result, if you believe the trend toward increasingly immersive and virtual worlds will continue in the coming decades, Roblox could be a fantastic long-term compounder for your portfolio.

10 stocks we prefer over Match Group

It pays to pay attention when our award-winning expert team makes a stock recommendation. After all, the Motley Fool Stock Advisor newsletter, which has been in circulation for nearly a decade, has tripled the market.

Match Group was not one of the top ten stocks for investors to buy right now, according to their list.

They do believe that these ten stocks are even better buys.

INVESTING IN VIRTUAL REAL ESTATE

Virtual real estate investing is frequently thought to be the domain of more seasoned real estate investors. However, this isn't entirely correct. With the coronavirus's influence on the US real estate market, virtual real estate investing is here to stay. It is not necessary to travel to other states to conduct property research. Furthermore, the purchase of an investment property is no longer limited by location. Thanks to real estate investment tools and real estate investor websites, anyone from anywhere can make profitable investment decisions.

What Is the Definition of Virtual Real Estate Investing?

Before purchasing an investment property, virtual real estate investing involves conducting property research and investment property analysis using real estate investment software. Instead of the traditional method of physically attending showings, it is essentially remote real estate investing. It is a cost-effective method of performing out-of-state real estate investing because it eliminates the need for travel and the associated costs and time.

Not to mention that it simplifies the process of scouting for offmarket properties, which frequently involves driving around neighbourhoods. Virtual real estate investors can do long-distance real estate investing from the comfort of their own homes.

How to Begin Investing in Virtual Real Estate

Becoming a real estate investor does not have to be difficult. If you have the necessary real estate resources, you can even start it as a side business for passive income. However, because you are no longer restricted to your city, virtual real estate investing opens up a plethora of options for any budget and investment objectives.

Buying rental property outside of your state may be more profitable. So, if you're ready to put this method to use, here's how to begin:

What Factors Influence the Selection of a Real Estate Market?

Because there are so many options to consider, long-distance real estate investing can be perplexing at first. If you're stuck for ideas, start with a state that interests you.

It could be a state with favorable Airbnb regulations or an ideal location for a vacation rental. If you're looking for typical rental properties, it could also be a property with no rent control and a large population. Then consider whether any cities or towns within it might be of interest to long-term tenants or tourists. How did you come to that conclusion? If there are tourist attractions, sites, or natural features nearby, there will be visitors. You can look up market statistics online to see if there will be a demand for long-term rental homes, such as the number of renters, the price-to-rent ratio, and the state of the job market and economy.

Even with a little research, this stage can be difficult. As a result, virtual real estate investing necessitates the use of real estate investment instruments. Mashvisor, a real estate investment software, can tell you what's going on in each town's housing market. It collects data from various listing sites to almost completely automate your real estate market research. You can use Mashvisor's real estate heatmap to explore neighbourhoods in any city in the United States. Different types of neighbourhood data can be analysed:

• Traditional and Airbnb rental income • Listing price • Airbnb occupancy rate • Average rate of return on a rental property (in traditional and Airbnb cash on cash return)

As a result, you can quickly learn about the housing market in your desired area and determine whether it is a good place to invest in real estate. It also provides a graphical representation of the real estate market study. The heatmap enables you to look for items based on important criteria such as cash on cash return.

The map is filtered, and the corresponding neighbourhoods with high values are highlighted in green. You don't have to have visited the area to use this information – virtual real estate investing means you know more about the investment potential than the locals.

Making a Business Choice

Buying a rental property out of state and investing close to home have one thing in common: in both cases, you must conduct an investment property study before selecting a property for sale. This entails digging deeper into a property's financials to determine whether it would be a profitable investment. Mashvisor can help both traditional and virtual real estate investors in this regard. This analysis is performed for you by the platform, allowing you to compare alternative options. Here's a quick overview of what the automatic analysis entails:

Expenses and potential sources of funding Enter your mortgage or cash data into the investment property calculator to calculate expenses and return on investment. Utilities, insurance, property management fees, and HOA fees are all estimated based on previous property data in the area. As a result, you can see right away if a particular investment property for sale is a good fit for your real estate investing strategy.

This is a rental arrangement. Mashvisor reports rental income, cash flow, cap rate, cash on cash return, monthly expenses, and occupancy rate. Furthermore, you'll receive a handy side-by-side comparison of Airbnb vs. traditional renting to assist you in determining which rental plan is the most profitable.

Mashvisor's Investment Property Calculator

Examine the competition. Mashvisor provides a list of comparable rental homes in the area to make out-of-state real estate investing even easier. Furthermore, standard and Airbnb rental comps are available. Size, occupancy rate, and, for Airbnbs, the Airbnb nightly rate are all available, as are Airbnb ratings and reviews. As a result, you will be able to charge a reasonable rental fee.

Rental Comps from Mashvisor

Once you've found your ideal investment property, you can complete the sale remotely with some assistance. In most areas, you can hire a home inspection service to visit the property without you and provide you with peace of mind. Then, to continue working on the discussions and the offer, it would be advantageous to contact a local agency. This can be done quickly over the phone or via email (Mashvisor listings include all agents' contact information). Finally, there is a requirement for a digital signature. Many documents must be signed before the transaction can be completed, not to mention leases once ownership is obtained. Most counties now accept digitally signed documents, which will save you a lot of time and paper. After all, virtual real estate investing is a cutting-edge technology that shouldn't require a lot of paperwork.

METAVERSE VIRTUAL REAL ESTATE IS SUCCESSIVE.

One such virtual world, The Sandbox, is now leading the pack in terms of traders and sales. The Sandbox had the highest trading volume last week, with more than $86 million traded for land plot NFTs, while Decentraland came in second, with more than $15 million traded for land plot NFTs.

So, what is the growing allure of purchasing a virtual plot of land?

According to Hayden Hughes, CEO of crypto social trading platform Alpha Impact, NFTs and play-to-earn games like Axie Infinity by Vietnamese studio Sky Mavis have introduced an entire generation of individuals into shared online communities. Hughes stated that as these communities grow, members have a creative drive to express themselves by owning metaverse assets such as land.

"The rush to acquire land in the metaverse is being driven by creatives who sincerely want to express themselves, as well as speculators looking to profit." In contrast to the 2017 ICO [initial coin offering] bubble, the metaverse has widespread adoption and a thriving (albeit early) ecosystem. "Facebook / Meta isn't the market leader in this field," Hughes explained, "and the rebrand has drawn attention to the ecosystem."

According to DappRadar, the price of metaverse land is rising in tandem with the demand for metaverse experiences. Last week, five of the ten most expensive NFT transactions were metaverse land plot NFTs in various virtual worlds.

The top grosser, according to the data, was the Fashion Street Estate in Decentraland, which sold for 618.000 MANA, or $2.42 million. An Axie Genesis plot, on the other hand, the most valuable territory in yet another stand-alone metaverse game, sold for 550 Ethereum last month (ETH). According to the creators' tweet, this was the "greatest sale ever for a single piece of digital property," with 550 ETH worth $2.48 million as of December 3.

Among the games available are Axie Infinity, Denctraland, and Metaverse Gaming.

According to the Axie Infinity whitepaper, "Lucia, the Axie motherland, is divided into tokenized parcels of land that operate as residences and bases of action for its Axies." Plots can be improved over time with a range of resources and crafting ingredients gathered throughout the game."

According to the developer whitepaper, Lunacia consists of 90,601 plots of land represented as NFTs and is freely sellable by users. The Genesis property in question, on the other hand, is extremely valuable due to its scarcity: the game's 90,601 plots contain only 220 Genesis plots.

According to Grayscale Investments' recent research, this expansion of the "creative economy," also known as "play-to-earn," allows users to own their digital assets as NFTs, exchange them with others in the game, and occasionally transport them to other digital experiences.

As a result, projects such as Decentraland are creating an open-world metaverse in which users can log in to play games and earn MANA (Decentraland's native currency), which can be used to purchase NFTs such as LAND or collectibles), vote on economic governance, or build NFTs.

Furthermore, as a value proposition for their time spent in-game, this architecture provides users with significant interoperability between systems.

According to Matt Maximo, research analyst at Grayscale Investments and co-author of the report, land in the metaverse is an intriguing concept because traditional real estate is valued primarily based on proximity to shops, services, and other people – you're limited by the time it takes to travel from your home.

Players in several metaverses, including Decentraland, can teleport globally, making travel quick and unrelated to valuation. Given the market's infancy, many of the higher-priced sales have come from LAND lots in desirable locations, such as proximity to prominent metaverse attractions. "Investing in LAND is exciting, but it comes with the same risks as any other emerging market." The owners of LAND and MANA are motivated to keep the Decentraland map small and the number of parcels low, but "there will come a time when enlarging the map and producing more LAND to sell will benefit them more than the dilution of their property," he explained.

He went on to say that because LAND plots are nonfungible tokens, liquidity is much lower than with underlying tokens such as MANA.

"If you're in a hurry to sell, you may be forced to sell at a loss to the highest bidder, whereas if I have MANA, I can go to an exchange like Uniswap or Coinbase and make the sale instantly," he added.

Is There an Infinite Land in the Metaverse?

While the metaverse's expanding options have greatly incentivized property purchase as a means for players to stake their claim in a virtual environment, one potential issue is that land may be in infinite supply.

"As a result, predicting how much land will be worth in the future is difficult, and purchasing today could be considered a risky investment.

"If, for example, digital land becomes oversupplied, supply-demand economics kicks in and the price falls. However, for investors who want to be among the first to own land in the digital world, the sheer number of possibilities that the metaverse may offer may outweigh the risk." " Reeve Collins, the co-founder of BLOCKv and SmartMedia Technologies, told GOBankingRates.

According to Eduardo Erlo, marketing manager of blockchain-based encrypted messenger Status, the buying frenzy for digital real estate may cause a temporary slump. Erlo went on to say that because land in the metaverse is infinitely plentiful, paying a high price for it now might be a waste of money.

He suggested that one way to avoid the infinite abundance of digital land would be for some metaverses to have built-in scarcity regarding plots of land, similar to the built-in monetary investment scarcity offered by Bitcoin.

"It's still too early to know anything," he said, "but it's interesting to watch."

Grayscale estimates that the commercial opportunity for bringing any number of metaverses to life could be worth more than $1 trillion per year. Furthermore, revenue from virtual game worlds could reach $400 billion in 2025, up from $180 billion in 2020.

According to several experts, purchasing virtual land in the metaverse can be considered an investment.

According to Robert Powers, Vivid Labs' director of decentralized media, the metaverse — and the many metaverses within it — will deliver on promises and evolve into a dynamic virtual environment to which we will all contribute in some way.

Powers, on the other hand, told GOBankingRates that we are still in the early days of the emerging metaverse — or metaverses because there will likely be many, not just one — and that we should be wary of speculation that leads to the kind of rapid price increases that we are seeing right now in the digital land market "

This burst of innovation, on the other hand, holds enormous promise for what's to come in a more fully immersive digital environment." " "Perhaps these early digital land buyers are the digital equivalents of owning the Empire State Building or even New York City," he speculated.

Dan Patterson, the general partner at Sfermion, an NFT-focused investment firm, makes another point about the value of digital real estate.

"In these future worlds, each plot of digital real estate will be a 3-dimensional profile page that is fully userowned and

developed," he said, adding, "How much is the most popular
Instagram page worth?"

CHAPTER 6

CRYPTO'S ROLE IN THE METAVERSES

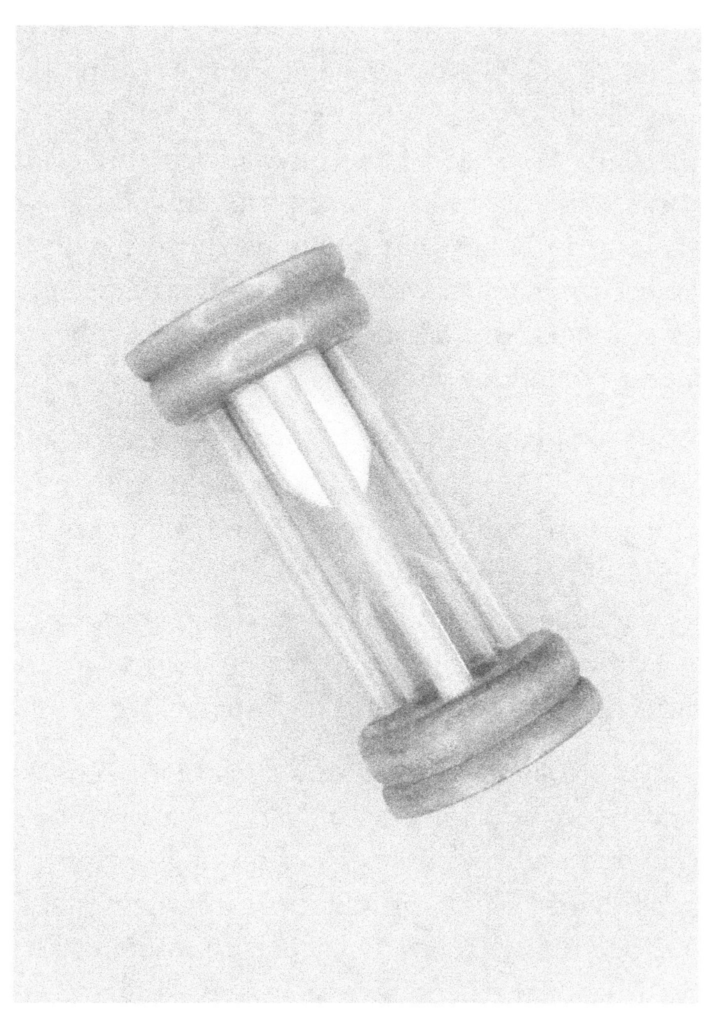

Crypto metaverse creators have frequently attempted to distinguish their worlds from previous iterations of metaverses in three critical ways:

Decentralization: In contrast to early virtual worlds, which were owned and controlled by corporations, crypto metaverses are frequently decentralized , with blockchain technology powering some or all metaverse game components. As a result, blockchain metaverses differ from the standard corporate structures and value extraction tactics used in today's game industry. Because of the unique structure of blockchain games, participants may have more equitable participation options. It also implies that individuals in the metaverse share metaverse ownership. Even if the original designers of the metaverse blockchain abandon the project, the game may continue to exist indefinitely.

User management: Decentralized autonomous organisations (DAOs) and governance tokens are used by crypto metaverses such as Decentraland to help put their users in charge of the game's future by allowing them to vote on changes and upgrades. As a result, metaverses can grow into entire communities with economies and democratic government, going beyond crypto games.

Crypto tokens, such as non-fungible tokens, are used to represent real-world objects in crypto metaverses (NFTs). Achievements and purchases can be quite useful to players in gaming contexts. NFTs provide in-game item standards with much-needed transparency and access to asset markets. Because each NFT is distinct, metaverse tokens and items could be designed to easily aid in the authentication of in-game usergenerated content as well as NFT gaming assets.

Crypto metaverses' economies are inextricably linked to the larger crypto economy because they use cryptocurrencies and blockchain infrastructure. Holders of metaverse currencies, avatar skins, and digital real estate can now trade them for real-world value on DEXs and NFT marketplaces.

Metaverse Games Can Be Both Financially and Socially Beneficial

While crypto metaverses (and NFT games in general) are still in their infancy, these new worlds hold enormous social and economic promise. Crypto metaverses can benefit users by providing new ways to play, invest, collect, and socialise, as well as new ways to earn money from it all. While work on the various metaverse platforms is notable, the numerous metaverse games can communicate and interoperate with one another, potentially transforming the nascent blockchain gaming ecosystem into a global economic pillar. Metaverse games, which combine the immersive environments of virtual reality, the addictive playability of social media and video games, and the value propositions of cryptocurrency, are poised to become a key feature of the internet's next phase.

NFTs: The Metaverse's Economy

How non-fungible tokens aid in the development of virtual world civilizations

A typical day in the metaverse — a shared immersive virtual reality — may soon resemble our familiar and beloved world. We will visit retail malls, travel across town, meet friends

97

in cafés, and exchange connections in ways that feel eerily real, thanks to significant advances in virtual reality and 5G communications.

For decades, metaverses have existed in the form of multiplayer internet games. However, we may soon enter an era of immersive experiences that are nearly indistinguishable from reality, ushering in new forms of interaction for both gamers and non-gamers.

Individuals settling the land, socialising socially, transferring goods, and asserting ownership rights can already be seen in prototype next-generation metaverses such as Decentraland and Somnium Space. A functioning economy, on the other hand, is required in any society (physical or virtual). The economy is based on digital properties being authenticated in the metaverse, such as one's metaverse home, automobile, farm, books, clothing, and furniture. To thrive, it must also be able to freely travel and trade between realms with different laws and rules.

Non-fungible tokens — blockchain-based records of digital ownership — will serve as the metaverse economy's backbone, allowing for the authentication of belongings, property, and even identity. Furthermore, because each NFT is protected by a cryptographic key that cannot be erased, copied, or destroyed, it allows for the reliable, decentralized verification of one's virtual identity and digital possessions that metaverse communities require in order to succeed and communicate with one another.

Beyond the hype of multi-million dollar digital art sales, the importance of NFTs may lie in their ability to foster the emergence of something resembling genuine human society in the metaverse, based on free markets (for goods, services, and ideas), autonomous ownership, and social contracts.

"NFTs initially concentrated on the digital art side of things.

However, it will be far more potent "Eric Anziani, COO of Crypto.com joins the team. "In the future, it will be the tool for representing any digital type of asset in virtual environments." As a result, the opportunities are limitless." "

Real estate development in a brave new world

Decentraland is filled with people conversing by fountains, shoppers in fashion boutiques, joggers on beach promenades, and casino croupiers luring guests to high-stakes poker.

These encounters are the result of virtual real estate development by individuals who have purchased land and built habitats that have piqued the interest of other Decentraland residents.

The experience is far from hyper-realistic (the Decentraland creators claim that the world is still in the "Iron Age"). Even in these early iterations, the potential is clear. People flock to interesting places in the metaverse, just as they do in real life. And, just like in Paris or Beverly Hills, celebrity automatically increases the value of the virtual real estate.

Land adjacency is a fundamental economic concept in Decentraland and other metaverses. All metaverse parcels are contiguous at a fixed point within finite geography. Scarcity arises as a result of the limited availability of the property. And scarcity allows property values to rise and fall in accordance with universal supply and demand laws.

A foundation is thus built for "a social experience with an economy driven by the existing layers of land ownership and content distribution," according to the Decentraland manifesto.

NFTs enable the property transactions that power the metaverse. These tokens provide unmistakable proof of ownership that is more secure than any land deed.

"Because of the way smart contracts are defined and NFTs are programmed, you simply cannot spoof metaverse property rights," Anziani explains. "You are aware that you have an asset and have the ability to establish complete ownership." You can then assert ownership rights based on the virtual environment's rules and conditions." "

Real estate for sale in London, New York, and Tokyo

The consequences of this real estate revolution are already being felt acutely. Republic Realm, a digital property investment fund, for example, paid nearly $900,000 for a plot of land in Decentraland in June. Republic Realm, which controls the investment fund Republic, is transforming the site into Metajuku, a virtual mall modelled after Tokyo's Harajuku district.

It won't be long before real estate investment trusts (REITs) begin spotting opportunities in the metaverse based on these behaviours. Property values in Decentraland rise and fall in lockstep with the economy.

This is exactly what its creators had in mind when they launched their virtual world in 2017.

"Decentraland's value proposition to application developers is that they may fully capitalise on the economic interactions between their programmes and users," according to the metaverse's manifesto.

To enable those economic connections, "the platform must facilitate the trading of three things: currency, products, and services."

Fashion was among the first industries to recognise the monetary value of NFTs and the metaverse. Burberry created NFT accessories for the video game Blankos Block Party, while Louis Vuitton released LOUIS THE GAME, its own NFT-studded video game.

Meanwhile, RTFKT, the metaverse's bespoke shoemaker, creates limited-edition NFT sneakers that can be worn in virtual worlds and have sold millions of dollars.

With so much momentum in the Iron Age of the metaverse, the virtual world's economic model based on NFT technology promises massive economies of scale.

"Only five months ago, we had 100 million crypto users worldwide." "We now have over 200 million users," Anziani claims. "We believe that metaverses – the combination of virtual worlds and blockchain technology – particularly NFTs – will be the next wave to reach a billion or two billion users."

IN 2022, INVEST IN THE TOP 11 METAVERSE CRYPTOCURRENCIES.

Consider a universe that isn't constrained by the facts of your life. You can work, play, relax, and communicate with people from all over the world in this alternate reality. You can go to parties, create amazing art, and amass a fortune. Anything is possible if you put your mind to it.

This isn't science fiction: it's the metaverse, and cryptocurrency is the key to getting into it.

Although Metaverse blockchain technology is still in its early stages, the concept of a digital universe has a long history. The metaverse is a concept developed by visionaries and science fiction writers who wish to travel beyond the physical constraints of our world in order to explore new frontiers and create new possibilities. The metaverse allows you to achieve new levels of digital success, explore new worlds, and interact with friends and family in novel ways.

Mark Zuckerberg is the most recent person to dabble in the metaverse, and he made a big deal out of it.

Despite the fact that Facebook, now known as Meta, is a large and powerful organisation, it is neither the first nor the last to be enamoured with the concept of the metaverse. After all, the metaverse is the next evolution of the internet, and neither the internet nor the metaverse can be controlled by a single corporation. Each corporation that participates, however, will have an impact not only on the architecture of the metaverse but also on how it will appear in the future.

What Exactly Is the Metaverse, and How Does It Function?

Neal Stephenson's cyberpunk novel Snow Crash introduced the metaverse in 1992 when he created a "metaverse." Stephenson defines a shared digital universe using virtual reality goggles and a common fiber optics network. His metaverse contains virtual replicas of everyday settings, ranging from parks and buildings to exotic and wildly amusing realms where only the rules and constraints of one's imagination apply.

Since Zuckerberg's introduction of the metaverse as "the next chapter of the internet," public interest in it has skyrocketed. This metaverse broadens your horizons by allowing you to do whatever you want, whether it's socialising, working, playing, purchasing, producing, or learning about new places and ideas. The metaverse not only puts the entire physical universe at your fingertips, but it also places the power of your mind in your hands.

You'll have your own virtual home in the metaverse and communicate with others via an online avatar that allows you to move, speak, and act freely. You'll have complete control over your life, including the ability to own virtual property in the same way that you can own real estate. You can even create a piece of property, such as art or a building, and sell it to other metaverse users in exchange for non-fungible tokens (NFTs) or other forms of payment.

NFTs are a type of collectible and in-game currency.

Users engage in play-to-earn models, exchanging virtual commodities or property for tokens, which serve as the foundation of their virtual economy.

They can also sell their metaverse cryptocurrency to other users or invest it in order to earn interest or collectibles.

Many of the most popular metaverse gaming sites have tokens that can be used for a variety of purposes or traded for real money in cryptocurrency or fiat currency.

Since Zuckerberg's announcement, the value of many NFTs and tokens has risen, and adopting metaverse crypto now can help you get in early on exchange-traded funds (ETFs) and ride a wave to metaverse success.

Top Cryptocurrencies in the Metaverse

To live, work, and play in another world, you'll need money, which you can get with bitcoin. There are numerous cryptocurrencies to choose from, as well as numerous metaverses to explore. Understanding the various options, distinctions, benefits, and drawbacks of each will assist you in making the best investment decision for your circumstances.

Mana Decentraland (MANA) Mana Decentraland Mana

Decentraland is an augmented reality platform where you can buy, sell, and manage virtual properties (called LAND). As a result, you have complete control over how you modify and expand your universe, and you can do so from the convenience of your phone, computer, or virtual reality (VR) headset. You'll need Decentraland MANA to get started. MANA is a native cryptocurrency that can be used to pay for goods and services, as well as to invest in real estate.

MANA is a well-known metaverse cryptocurrency with a large user base that appeals to even the most inexperienced users. The Decentraland metaverse also offers users exciting interactive activities such as concerts and festivals, as well as dynamic entertainment venues comparable to those found in the real world. Decentraland is expanding and has a thriving development team, giving you a wide range of options and possibilities. MANA increased 400 percent to a record high of $4.16 after Facebook announced its name change to meta, which prompted increased interest in virtual property tokens.

Despite their popularity, MANA and Decentraland have some drawbacks. MANA is built on the Ethereum metaverse blockchain, which has high gas costs but high security. Users rarely encounter another user "out in the wild," making the experience lonely. There's not much to do, and the scenery is monotonous. Decentraland tokens can be used in a variety of ways, and the platform is constantly updated to add new features and possibilities. The community is overseen by the Security Advisory Board, and both LAND and NFTs can be auctioned.

Purchase and Trade MANA on the spot/derivatives

The Playground (SAND)

The Jungle of the Sandbox Biome

The Sandbox is a virtual world in which users can buy and sell virtual land and other items with SAND, metaverse money. You can use the power of SAND cryptocurrency to build and modify anything you can imagine, while also selling your virtual experience.

SoftBank, one of the world's most powerful digital investment firms, has backed the Sandbox. As a result, you can buy, sell, and stake your virtual plots and valuables. Furthermore, the Sandbox is a play-to-learn metaverse that allows you to personalise your experience. You can, among other things, create your own game, play other games, own virtual land, and gather, construct, or control real estate.

The Sandbox's metaverse is based on the Ethereum blockchain, which ensures maximum safety and security. This does, however, imply that you may have to pay exorbitant gasoline prices on occasion. Nonetheless, its editor allows you to create unrivalled animations and models while also providing powerful tools for creating the virtual world you desire.

Buy and sell SAND on Bybit Spot/Derivatives. Market

Atlas of the Stars (ATLAS)

Solana-powered Star Atlas

With Star Atlas, you can expand your experience beyond the realm of the tangible. The sky is the limit here, and you have complete freedom to explore an infinite number of possibilities. You can, for example, explore a unique metaverse on your spacecraft, join or start a faction, and create your own planet.

This one-of-a-kind reality is powered by ATLAS, a metaverse token. It is the key to exciting new vistas and possibilities, and it is powered by the Solana metaverse blockchain. The Solana metaverse blockchain is similar to Ethereum in terms of speed, safety, and security, but it is more scalable and less expensive. ATLAS metaverse currencies can be used to purchase any digital assets required to immerse yourself in the Star Atlas universe, including ships, land, crew members, and equipment. You can also use ATLAS to buy POLIS, an in-game currency that will assist you in certain game areas.

POLIS, in particular, will be charged with administering and controlling your new planet through the issuance of decrees.

While the Star Atlas metaverse is a novel concept with a valuable metaverse token, the two tokens — ATLAS and POLIS — may be confusing or frustrating to some.

Nonetheless, the advantages outweigh the disadvantages, and Star Atlas is a vibrant, engaging environment with NFTs that provide a lot of virtual bang for the buck.

Infinite Axie (AXS)

In-game pets for Axie

Axie Infinity is played by over a quarter of a million people every day. Players own AXS tokens, which give them a stake in the game's ownership and operation.

Players can create kingdoms, seek out rare resources, and build treasure chests. The metaverse blockchain rewards the most active players.

Axes are non-fungible tokens (NFTs) that can be purchased and traded outside of the game. Axes can range in price from $150 to over $100,000 depending on their rarity. In contrast, the most expensive Axie was sold for 300 ETH, and Axie Infinity set the record for the highest-ever $1 billion in trading in August. It is available on a variety of platforms, including iOS, Android, Windows, and Mac.

Because AXS, like many other metaverse coins, is built on the Ethereum metaverse blockchain, gas fees can be quite high. You may, however, have faith in the platform's safety and security. Furthermore, AXS can be exchanged for other cryptocurrencies such as Ether or fiat money.

Players can earn AXS by completing quests and other platform activities, but the number of AXS they can earn per day is limited. Furthermore, some of these activities necessitate a significant time commitment, making full participation difficult for those with jobs or other responsibilities. Finally, while playing the game allows you to earn AXS, it is not free. Because players must have at least three Axies to participate, the initial prices may be prohibitively expensive for many.

Purchase and trade AXS/USDT on the spot

Aliens and Their Worlds (TLM)

Aliens World CC: The official website of Alien Worlds.

Alien Worlds is a DeFi Decentralized Finance (DeFi) brings the decentralized concept of blockchain to the world of finance. Build...

A blockchain-based metaverse and game in which participants compete for scarce resources within the community. Alien World has decentralized components, and players can take things a step further by staking Trillium (TLM) and gaining voting rights in the Planet DAO.

As an open-source blockchain ledger, decentralized Autonomous Organization (DAO) is governed by a set of principles.

Anyone who wishes to participate must have a WAX Cloud Wallet. They can start mining after logging into Alien Worlds and receiving TLM money. These tokens can be used to run for president of one or more Alien World planets' governments.

NFTs can also be earned and used to perform tasks, fight other players, or mine TLM. TLM can be used to mine NFTs, acquire or upgrade certain objects, and participate in missions and in-game activities in addition to regulating the Alien Worlds metaverse. Through TLM, the most active users are rewarded. TLM can also be traded for Ethereum, WAX, or BSC.

Low initial costs and the possibility of earning bitcoin through gameplay are luring new players to this game.

However, some users may find its user interface to be overly simplistic.

TLM/USDT Perpetual Trade Only on Bybit Enjin (ENJ)

Users of the Enjin platform can create, store, and sell virtual goods. To begin, developers must create a smart contract that assigns value to their virtual goods using ENJ tokens, the metaverse token. Players can then trade, sell, or use virtual goods in accordance with the terms of the contract. The merchant receives ENJ when an item is sold.

ENJ, like all other metaverse coins, is in short supply.

There will only be one billion produced and distributed. ENJ can be stored in the platform's wallet, which links all of the platform's functions. The wallet can be used to access and use content, exchange things and metaverse currency, and sell digital commodities for ENJ.

Enjin also provides a distinct marketplace experience, allowing users and businesses to broaden their markets by utilising NFTs and QR codes and interacting with other users via websites, apps, and games. The network is Ethereum-powered and provides a decentralized experience. However, because the wallet is not open-source, vetting it can be difficult. Furthermore, ENJ is not backed by any asset, profit, or commodity.

Buy and trade ENJ on Bybit's Spot/Derivatives market. Market

Illuvium (ILV)

Illuvium is an open-world role-playing game (RPG) that allows players to explore a large and beautiful area. They travel through the land of Illuvium, completing chores, discovering animals known as Illuvials, and delving into the mystery that surrounds it.

Over 100 Illuvials must be gathered, each with their own set of abilities, classes, strengths, and weaknesses. When you find an Illuvial, you have the option of keeping it, upgrading it, or storing it in your player wallet. NFTs include illuvials, skins, and other collectibles that can be traded in-game or on third-party platforms such as the Illuvium decentralized market (IlluvDEX).

Illuvium is a cryptocurrency that runs on the Ethereum network and employs the ILV, a native ERC-20 token. Illuvium, on the other hand, does not require the use of ILV to play. Despite the importance of the ILV in the game's structure, the game is available for free in many locations, with a premium paid subscription option. Token holders can use ILV for liquidity mining and governance. ILV tokens can be obtained by completing certain objectives, such as missions.

ILV distribution and staking illuvium

The price of ILV may fluctuate due to speculation and blockchain usage. As a result, only ten million ILV will be distributed, with three million reserved for staking incentives. The circulating supply refers to the number of cryptocurrencies or tokens that are publicly available and circulating in the cryptocurrency market...

As the price of ILV falls, the price of ILV may rise. While ILV grants you access to the game and its features, there are some drawbacks, such as high gas fees on the Ethereum network. Despite the fact that Illuvium has yet to be released, the hype surrounding this metaverse game is already overwhelming. Illuvium will be released in theatres in 2022.

On Bybit, you can trade the Trending ILV/USDT Perpetual.

The Gala Games (GALA)

Gala Games is a gaming environment that gives players complete control over their gameplay. Players can keep their NFTs, which aid in various gaming tasks, or they can sell, trade, or gift them to other players. Furthermore, gala Games provides several NFTs, such as the CraneBot, that can be used in the game for which they were created as well as other games in the same ecosystem.

Gala Games, like other metaverse games, has its own native token called the GALA. The GALA is a cryptographically secure currency that serves as the primary medium of exchange among participants. GALA rewards both nodes and players, with tokens incentivizing nodes and top players gaining tokens for their efforts.

Players can also use GALA to participate in the governance of Gala Games, giving them near-unprecedented power over the content and development of new games.

Despite the fact that Gala Games is still in its early stages, the development team has established clear objectives and a road map to achieve them. The GALA token has a lot of room for growth, and the game platform is hard at work on several new titles that will be released soon. In order to motivate players and nodes, GALA tokens and NFT awards are used.

One of Gala Games' most appealing features is its free games. Players who register an account incur no costs, fees, or subscriptions.

Customers may encounter significant gas prices when transferring currencies or completing transactions due to Gala Games' use of the Ethereum network.

GALA/USDT Perpetual Trade on Bybit

Blockchain Flow (FLOW)

Flow is a blockchain network for developers that allows for the creation of various apps, games, and digital assets. Its multi-node, multi-role architecture scales without sharding and concentrates individual node functions for faster, more efficient performance. Furthermore, flow ensures that its users' data is kept private and secure while also providing them with digital assets that can be traded on the open market.

Smart contracts written in Cadence, a programming language that is safer and easier to use for crypto users, are another distinguishing feature of the Flow network.

Consumers benefit from efficient, user-friendly payment on-ramps, while developers benefit from a wide range of tools and built-in support. Flow uses a proof-of-stake (PoS) consensus mechanism with validation distributed across multiple nodes. Transaction validation necessitates the participation of each type of node.

Flow's multi-role architecture distinguishes it from the competition, allowing the network to scale without sharding.

Because Flow was designed specifically to support crypto games and NFT collectibles, interaction opportunities may be limited at first. Users can purchase NFTs on the market or through other apps, and they can even trade digital goods through NBA Top Shot. Developers have access to a variety of built-in tools that make it easy to create DApps or simply experiment.

The FLOW token is Flow's native coin. FLOW rewards validators and the token serves as a payment method. As a result, FLOW is the money that powers the network and supports the ecosystem of apps that run on top of it.

Trade Perpetual FLOW/USDT on Bybit

WEMIX

WEMIX is a blockchain platform that is used for gaming as well as other purposes. Users can win or create goods for NFTs, then trade them with other users and trade WEMIX tokens. WEMIX, from Wemade Tree Pte. Ltd., is a newcomer to the sector, providing consumers with a decentralized marketplace to spend and exchange digital currency.

WEMIX, which can also be purchased on cryptocurrency exchanges with Bitcoin, Ethereum, and other cryptocurrencies, can be easily converted into game tokens.

On Bybit NetVRk, you can trade the trending pair WEMIX/USDT.

NetVRk tokens, like other metaverse tokens, provide users with access to virtual assets such as real estate, homes, automobiles, and other commodities. You can also use tokens to buy advertising space, which generates passive income and allows you to accumulate more tokens and expand your universe. You can also use the token to purchase a stake in the NetVRk, which will pay you a predetermined interest rate based on how many metaverse tokens you stake with the network.

The NetVRk metaverse, with an infinite number of unique content, allows all users to develop and create the virtual world of their dreams. Furthermore, the site offers a plethora of opportunities for new experiences and relationships with other users, as well as monetary prizes for participation.

While the possibilities are appealing, there are a few drawbacks to consider. NetVRk is built on the Ethereum network, which has high gas and other fees. NetVRk is also a newer platform than some others, so some kinks may need to be worked out.

Is Crypto the Metaverse's Password?

NFTs and crypto will eventually be the keys to gaining access to the virtual world of the metaverse. NFTs can be used to gain access to digital assets such as virtual homes and businesses, as well as virtual clothes, art, and other goods. Your NFTs are protected by the metaverse blockchain, which prevents them from being duplicated or hacked.

Although metaverse blockchain technology is well-established, the metaverse as a whole is still in its early stages, so it hasn't yet taken shape. Furthermore, while much speculation exists as to what that may entail, the value of non-fungible tokens remains a significant source of uncertainty. Nonetheless, many NFTs, including those listed below, have demonstrated their growth and potential, which is why they are becoming more popular as an investment option.

The metaverse can open up a world of possibilities, but the real promise is held by the user. You can profit from digital assets by monetizing your digital crafts.

Fundraisers, games, and collectibles can all be converted into digital assets that can then be tokenized as in-game assets or made into play-to-earn games. Users can invest in and trade non-fungible exchange tokens to earn real money without ever playing a game. It is even possible to build a virtual reality that is identical to our own and improve on key aspects of it. However, using a metaverse blockchain that secures and certifies the data it contains as well as the money that supports it is critical. Finally, the best cryptocurrency for the future allows you to enter the world of your choice.

CHAPTER 7

BEST METAVERSE GAMES TO PLAY IN 2022

The "Metaverse" has gained popularity in recent months, but it's not too late to get involved. Here is a list of the best Metaverse games to play in 2022.

NFT games have been around for a long time. There were quite a few in the early days of crypto. However, it all started with the huge success of Axie Infinity earlier this year.

Following the meteoric rise of Axie Infinity, other crypto games followed suit, with investors looking for the next "moon"

NFT game. Many people believe the "Metaverse" will be the next big thing.

The Metaverse is a collection of virtual worlds that exist even when you're not actively playing the game (s). Most of these virtual environments are linked with VR and AR to increase immersion, but they are not limited to these technologies.

Most Metaverse games necessitate the possession of one-of-a-kind, fully digital NFTs. The goal of Metaverse is to connect our physical and digital worlds. It is thought to be the next generation of the internet.

Facebook has recently changed its name to "Meta" and has devoted itself entirely to the growth and advancement of the Metaverse. As a result, many businesses have begun to follow Facebook's lead and pay more attention to the Metaverse.

This is why many people believe the Metaverse will be a huge thing in a few years and are starting to invest large sums of money in it. As a result, in 2022, we set out to find the best Metaverse games to play.

Top 15 Metaverse Games in 2022

Here are some of our picks for the best Metaverse games in 2022. These are the games that we think will be relevant and stable in 2022.

1 Infinite Axie (AXS)

The first name on the list is Axie Infinity. Axie Infinity was released in 2018, but its popularity has recently increased.

People have made a lot of money from the game, which has become a mainstay in the NFT gaming industry.

Axie Infinity was inspired by Pokémon. It has creatures called "Axies" that you can use to fight other Axies. It now has a $9 billion market cap, making it the most valuable Metaverse game. It is currently the best and most popular Metaverse game, and its creators have high hopes for it.

2 The Game of Sandbox (SAND)

The Sandbox is a community-driven platform where you can play, develop, own, and manage a virtual plot of land. As long as you own that piece of LAND, you can pretty much do whatever you want in The Sandbox Game, just like in any other sandbox game.

You can also create your own NFT avatar and play or explore other people's LANDs. The game's style and feel are strikingly similar to Minecraft due to its block-like graphics.

Among the companies that have worked with it in the alpha testing phase are Atari, Care Bears, The Smurfs, Snoop Dogg, The Walking Dead, and Adidas. Collaborations with these companies have helped the Sandbox Game become one of the best Metaverse games to play and keep an eye on in the future.

3 Decentraland (MANA) is yet another cryptocurrency that has recently risen and reached new all-time highs.

Decentraland is the first completely decentralized world. It's similar to The Sandbox Game in that you can play, create, build, explore, and do a variety of other things.

119

To get started with Decentraland, all you need is a digital wallet like Metamask and your favourite web browser. Following that, you can begin exploring Decentraland's digital world, participating in events, and interacting with other users.

4 Illuvium (ILV)

Illuvium is an open-world role-playing game based on blockchain technology. You can explore the vast environment of the game and capture powerful monsters known as "Illuvials." Despite the fact that the game has yet to be released, it already has a $1 billion market cap and is one of the top Metaverse games available.

So far, the developers have shown off samples of the Illuvium gameplay experience, and it has been nothing short of spectacular. It has beautiful graphics, a vibrant setting, and fluid gameplay. Of course, only time will tell if Illuvium truly is a masterpiece. Even so, if the clips are accurate, it has the potential to be the best Metaverse game.

5 UFO Games (UFO)

UFO Gaming is another Metaverse project to keep an eye on in 2022. It's a full-fledged Metaverse ecosystem, with each planet representing a unique game. The play-to-earn strategy will be used in all of their games.

Their first game is called Super Galactic. It's a game with in-game tasks, tournaments, and PVP war modes where you can earn money. There's also a breeding and trading system, as well as an NFT marketplace for items, weapons, and characters. In the future, UFO Gaming should release more games.

6 Forged by Vulcan (PYR)

Vulcan Forged, a game collection, is also part of the Metaverse. Vulcan Verse, Berserk, Forge Arena, Vulcan Chess, and Blockbabies are the four games that are currently available. Four more are in the works, however: Block Babies, Coddle Pets, Geocats, and Agora.

Each game has its own gameplay as well as NFTs that can be used or traded in the market. Vulcan Forged is the most rapidly expanding blockchain game and decentralized application platform. It was one of the first established game studios in the Metaverse. It can also create some of the best games in the Metaverse.

7 Mobox (MBOX)

Mobox is a free-to-play game that allows you to earn rewards simply by playing. It combines DeFi and gaming to create an ecosystem in which everyone can enjoy the same universe.

The "MOMOverse" is expanding by the day, with features like a marketplace, NFT farming, and several games now available, with more on the way. The MOMOverse has MOMO Avatars, MOMO NFTs, and even a physical Blind Box that can be transferred to the digital world by scanning the attached QR code.

8 Atlas of the Stars (ATLAS)

Star Atlas is a one-of-a-kind space exploration strategy game in which you can take one of three paths. On this list, it is the first Metaverse game built on the Solana blockchain.

Although the game is still in development, it has already become one of the most popular Metaverse games on the Solana blockchain.

The game's visuals will be stunning because it is powered by Unreal Engine 5. Explore the galaxy's depths and seize control of various territories. Furthermore, Star Atlas provides a unique multiplayer experience, allowing you to explore the galaxy with your friends.

9. Polkadots (POLC)

Polkacity is a 3D and augmented reality platform, as are the majority of the games on this list. It's also the first NFT platform and game to support multiple blockchains in 3D and augmented reality.

Polkacity supports the Ethereum and Binance blockchains, as well as a bridge that allows POLC to be transferred from Ethereum to Binance.

Polkacity is an exciting game to watch. The game isn't yet available, but according to their schedule, the first version should be available in the fourth quarter of 2021. The creators of the game call it "the GTA of crypto," and it's a promising Metaverse idea for 2022.

10. Revomon (REVO)

Revomon is a game similar to Axie Infinity in which players collect, breed, battle, and trade Revomons.

This Metaverse game offers an immersive virtual reality experience in which you can explore a digital world populated by various Revomons.

123

It's a game where you can have fun while also earning cryptocurrency. The beta version is now available for download from the company's website. In Revomon, you can choose between Gorlit, Deksciple, and Zorelle as your companions as you explore the Revomon realm.

11. MondMondMondMondMondMon (SMON)

StarMon is a 3D NFT play-to-earn game with a variety of monsters each with its own special abilities. It features battles with various trainers on Andres Land, an adventure mode for earning uncommon goodies, and the ability to breed different Starmons to start your own collection.

In addition to the unique Starmon creatures, you can acquire Starmon Lands and create unique Starmon NFT avatars. They'll also release Starmon Go, a Pokémon GO-like app in which your phone acts as a gateway between the real world and the Starmon Metaverse.

12. Bloktopia (BLOK)

Bloktopia is a virtual reality platform built on the Polygon blockchain that promises to provide the cryptocurrency community with a one-of-a-kind VR experience. Think of Bloktopia as a skyscraper that serves as a central hub for all of your crypto adventures. Bloktopia allows you to make money by playing games, selling real estate, advertising, and other means.

You'll see a completely virtual environment through the eyes of a first-person perspective. Bloktopia allows you to relax, communicate, play games, and do other things. It's more than just a game; it's an entirely new world in virtual reality. Bloktopia is still in its early stages, but it has a lot planned for 2022, making it an excellent Metaverse game to keep an eye on.

13. Monster Hunt on Blockchain (BCMC)

Blockchain Monster Find is a blockchain-based game similar to Pokémon GO in which players hunt and battle monsters. It is the first NFT game to run entirely on the blockchain, as well as the first to exist across multiple blockchains.

It adheres to the same set of rules as the majority of Pokémon-inspired games. You must hunt and collect various creatures in order to use them in battles with other players. It's a free play-to-earn game that allows players to start with no money and on a variety of blockchains.

Blockchain Monster Hunt now supports the Ethereum, BSC, Polygon, and Ambros blockchains, with plans to add Heco and Moonriver in the future.

14. SolChicks (CHICKS)

SolChicks is an amazing fantasy game built on the Solana blockchain. It's currently the most popular fantasy game on Solana. Despite the fact that the token is not yet publicly available, it already has a community of over 500K users.

It features both PvP and PvE action, as well as a MOBA-style experience with a wide range of talents and powers. SolChicks have distinct abilities, stats, and cute little costumes that you will manage and employ. If it continues on its current trajectory, it has the potential to become the best Metaverse game on the Solana network.

15. Sword of Ember (EMBER)

Ember Sword is a sandbox MMORPG with an engrossing storey and a rewarding progression system. It features a fast-paced combat system with distinct classes and abilities. Like most MMORPGs, the game has PvE and PvP modes. The best part about Ember Sword is that it is entirely free to play and can be accessed via browsers or their client.

It is still in the early stages of development and in pre-alpha. The developers plan to make alpha testing available to the public in 2022, and they are currently working on fine-tuning gameplay components. Nonetheless, Ember Sword appears to be a potential Metaverse game that could be a good long-term investment. It's one of the riskier items on this list, but it appears to be a promising Metaverse game that could be a good long-term investment.

Before we proceed, keep in mind that none of this is financial advice. The cryptocurrency market, including the Metaverse, is extremely volatile, with values fluctuating at all times. As a result, always invest only what you can afford to lose and (DYOR) do your homework.

Having said that, the top Metaverse games to play in 2022 are the ones listed above. We believe that by 2022, these games will have dominated the Metaverse market and will thrive in the years to come.

Some of our suggestions are well-known and well-established, whereas others are brand new and still in the works. So pick your favourite and enjoy your time in the Metaverse.

CHAPTER 8

THE ALTCOIN

Alternative Cryptocurrencies (Altcoins): What Are They?

Altcoins are cryptocurrencies that exist in addition to Bitcoin (BTCUSD). They share some similarities with Bitcoin, but they differ significantly. Some altcoins, for example, build blocks or validate transactions using a different consensus technique. Furthermore, they may be able to differentiate themselves from Bitcoin by offering new or improved features such as smart contracts or lower price volatility.

As of November 2021, there are approximately 14,000 cryptocurrencies. According to CoinMarketCap, Bitcoin and Ether alone accounted for roughly 60% of the total cryptocurrency market in November 2021. 1 The remainder was comprised of so-called altcoins. Because they are frequently derived, altcoin price movements tend to follow Bitcoin's path. Analysts believe that as cryptocurrency investing ecosystems mature and new markets for these coins emerge, price fluctuations for altcoins will become independent of Bitcoin trading signals.

AN INTRODUCTION TO ALTERNATIVE CRYPTOCURRENCIES

All Bitcoin alternatives are referred to as "altcoins." It is a mash-up of the words "alternative" and "coin." Bitcoin and altcoins have very similar core designs. As a result, they share code and operate similarly to peer-to-peer systems or as a large computer capable of simultaneously processing massive amounts of data and transactions. In some cases, altcoins aim to be the next Bitcoin by becoming a low-cost digital transaction medium.

However, there are significant differences between Bitcoin and altcoins. Bitcoin was one of the first cryptocurrencies, and its philosophy and design served as a template for subsequent coins.

However, its implementation has significant flaws.

Proof of work (PoW), for example, is a time-consuming and energy-intensive consensus technique used to build blocks. Bitcoin's smart contract capabilities are also limited.

Following its launch in 2009, Bitcoin became the first widely used proof of work application. (PoW).

Many other cryptocurrencies are built on 2 PoW, which enables secure, decentralized consensus.

Altcoins capitalise on Bitcoin's perceived flaws to gain a competitive advantage. Several altcoins use the proof of stake (PoS) consensus technique to reduce energy consumption and the time it takes to build blocks and process new transactions.

Ether, the world's second-largest cryptocurrency by market capitalization, is used in Ethereum smart contracts as gas (or payment for transaction costs).

As the much-anticipated release of Ethereum 2.0 has demonstrated, altcoins frequently address previous criticisms of Bitcoin, such as scalability and sustainability.

By separating themselves from Bitcoin in this way, altcoins have created a market for themselves. As a result, they've drawn the attention of investors who see them as viable Bitcoin alternatives. Investors expect to profit as altcoins gain popularity and users, and their prices rise.

ALTCOINS COME IN DIFFERENT FLAVORS AND CATEGORIES, DEPENDING ON THEIR FUNCTIONS AND CONSENSUS PROCESSES.

Here's a rundown of some of the most important:

130

Mining-based

Mining-based altcoins are created through the mining process. PoW is a mechanism by which systems generate new money by solving difficult problems in order to build blocks, which is used by the majority of mining-based altcoins. Altcoins based on mining include Litecoin, Monero, and ZCash. The majority of the leading cryptocurrencies were mining-based in early 2020. Premined altcoins are a popular alternative to mining-based altcoins and are frequently included in initial coin offerings (ICOs) (ICO). Before being listed on cryptocurrency exchanges, these coins are distributed rather than manufactured using an algorithm. Ripple's XRP token is an example of a pre-mined coin.

Stablecoins

Volatility has characterised cryptocurrency trading and usage since its inception. Stablecoins attempt to reduce overall volatility by tying their value to a basket of goods such as fiat currencies, precious metals, or other cryptocurrencies. The basket is intended to serve as a backup for holders in the event that the coin fails or has problems. Stable coin price fluctuations should not exceed a certain threshold.

Tether's USDT, MakerDAO's DAI, and the USD Coin are all well-known stablecoins (USDC). Visa Inc. (V) announced in March 2021 that it would begin settling select transactions on its network in USDC via the Ethereum blockchain, with plans to expand stable coin settlement capacity later that year.

Tokens of Security

Security tokens are similar to stock market securities, with the exception that they are digital in nature. Security tokens, like traditional equities, often provide holders with equity in the form of ownership or a dividend distribution. The possibility of such tokens appreciating is a strong incentive for investors to invest in them.

Exodus, a Bitcoin wallet company, completed an SEC-qualified Reg A+ token sale in 2021, selling $75 million in common stock converted to Algorand tokens.

Because this is the first instance of digital asset security. It is a historical event to offer equity in a US-based issuing corporation.

Coins of Meme

Meme coins, as the name implies, are based on a joke or a humorous parody of other well-known cryptocurrencies. They frequently gain popularity quickly, with well-known crypto influencers and everyday investors looking for quick profits promoting them online.

Elon Musk, the CEO of Tesla Inc. (TSLA) and a cryptocurrency enthusiast, for example, regularly sends out cryptic tweets about popular meme coins like Dogecoin (DOGEUSD) and Shiba Inu, which can have a significant impact on their pricing. For example, when Musk shared a photo of his Shiba Inu puppy, Floki, riding in a Tesla in October 2021, Shiba rose 91 percent in 24 hours. 6 Hundreds of these cryptocurrencies posted large percentage gains solely on speculation during the massive run-up in these specific altcoins during April and May 2021, dubbed "meme coin season" by many.

The cryptocurrency industry's equivalent of an initial public offering (IPO) is an initial coin offering (ICO) (IPO). An initial coin offering (ICO) is a method for a company to raise funds for the development of a new coin, app, or service.

Tokens of Utility

Utility tokens are used to provide services across a network.

They could be used to pay for services, network expenses, or to redeem prizes, for example. Utility tokens, unlike security tokens, do not pay dividends or require an ownership stake. To purchase network storage space, a utility token such as Filecoin is used.

Are Altcoins a Good Investment?

The altcoin industry is still in its infancy. It's a one-sided game. In the previous decade, the number of altcoins listed on cryptocurrency exchanges exploded, attracting swarms of ordinary investors looking to profit from price fluctuations. Such investors, on the other hand, lack the capital required to generate significant market liquidity. Furthermore, altcoin prices are vulnerable to quicksilver fluctuations due to a lack of regulation and thin marketplaces.

Consider Ethereum's ether, which peaked at $1,299.95 on January 12, 2018. After a few weeks, it fell to $597.36, and by the end of the year, it had dropped to $89.52.

133

However, just two years later, in November 2021, the altcoin reached new highs of nearly $4,750. Traders who use timed transactions have the potential to make a lot of money.

However, there is a problem. Cryptocurrency markets are still in their infancy. Despite repeated attempts, there are no formal investment criteria or indicators for cryptocurrencies. Speculation is the primary driver of the altcoin market. There are numerous examples of dead cryptocurrencies that failed to gain popularity or vanished after collecting investor funds.

As a result, investors willing to accept the enormous risk of operating in an unregulated and volatile market may be interested in altcoins. They should also be able to deal with the stress that comes with significant price changes.

Cryptocurrency markets can provide excellent returns for such investors.

Pros

Altcoins are "better versions" of Bitcoin that aim to address the flaws of the cryptocurrency.

Stablecoins, like altcoins, have the potential to fulfil Bitcoin's original promise as a daily transaction medium.

Certain cryptocurrencies, such as Ethereum's ether and Cardano's ADA, have already gained widespread acceptance, resulting in high prices.

Investors can choose from a wide variety of altcoins, each of which serves a specific purpose in the crypto economy.

Cons

The investment market for altcoins is much smaller than that of Bitcoin. As of November 2021, Bitcoin holds a 42 percent stake in the global cryptocurrency market.

Due to a lack of regulation and established investment criteria, the altcoin market has fewer investors and limited liquidity. As a result, their prices are more volatile than Bitcoin's.

It's not always easy to tell the difference between altcoins and their various applications, which complicates and perplexes investment decisions.

Several "dead" cryptocurrencies have depleted investor capital.

The Future of Altcoins

The events that led to the adoption of a nationally printed dollar in the nineteenth century served as a model for discussions about the future of altcoins and, indeed, cryptocurrencies. During this time, various types and types of local currencies circulated throughout the United States. Each had a distinct personality and was accompanied by a one-of-a-kind instrument. For example, gold certificates were backed by Treasury gold holdings. The government-backed the US notes used to fund the Civil War.

Local banks also printed their own currency, which was sometimes backed by fictitious reserves. The variety of currencies and financial instruments reflects the current state of cryptocurrency markets. There are thousands of cryptocurrencies available on today's markets, each claiming to serve a specific purpose and market.

According to the current state of the altcoin markets, the emergence of a single cryptocurrency appears unlikely. However, the majority of the more than 1,800 altcoins listed on cryptocurrency exchanges are unlikely to survive. Instead, the cryptocurrency industry will be dominated by a small number of cryptocurrencies with superior usability and use cases.

Altcoins are a low-cost way for investors to broaden their horizons in the cryptocurrency markets beyond Bitcoin. Profits from cryptocurrency market rallies have been several times greater than profits from Bitcoin.

However, there are risks to investing in altcoins, not the least of which is a lack of regulation. As the bitcoin market matures, more expertise and capital will undoubtedly enter, paving the way for regulation and reducing volatility.

Altcoins are an excellent choice for investors looking to diversify their portfolios within the crypto markets, as they generate returns that are typically multiples of Bitcoin.

What Exactly Is an Alternate Currency (Altcoin)?

Altcoins are cryptocurrencies that are similar to Bitcoin (and sometimes also other than Ether). These coins distinguish themselves from Bitcoin by improving their capabilities and addressing their flaws.

What Are the Top 10 Cryptocurrencies?

As of November 2021, the top ten altcoins are Ethereum, Binance Coin (BNB), Tether (USDT), Solana, Cardano, XRP, Polkadot, Dogecoin, USD Coin, and Shiba Inu.

How Much Does an Altcoin Cost?

Altcoins can be purchased for as little as a few pennies or as much as hundreds of dollars. In November 2021, Ethereum, for example, was trading at around $4,500, while Ripple's XRP, the sixth most valuable cryptocurrency, was trading at $1.10.87.

Which altcoin is the best to invest in?

By market capitalization, Ether is the largest and most well-known altcoin.

It is a component of Ethereum, one of the most complex blockchain platforms in recent memory, and its smart contract capabilities have demonstrated use cases.

Are Altcoins a Good Investment?

Many of the same investment risks apply to altcoins as they do to Bitcoin. In addition, many minor altcoins are illiquid.

Well-known altcoins such as ether and XRP, on the other hand, compete with Bitcoin.

Last Thoughts

Altcoins are a great way for cryptocurrency investors to diversify their holdings. Though some are well-known, such as Ethereum's ether, the vast majority of the more than 10,000 altcoins available have yet to make an impact. Altcoins are an excellent example of how cryptocurrencies can disrupt traditional finance. Investors should, however, do their homework before investing in them. The risks of investing in altcoins are comparable to, if not greater than, those of Bitcoin.

CHAPTER 9

BITCOIN AND ALTCOIN INVESTMENT STRATEGIES

A collection of strategies and pointers to get you started with cryptocurrency investing.

We go over some basic strategies for investing in Bitcoin and other cryptocurrencies. All of the strategies listed below are viable options for investing in the volatile cryptocurrency market.

TIP: These are completely legal and above-board white-hat investing and trading strategies. This is not investment advice, but rather educational and informative content aimed at understanding the fundamentals.

Furthermore, this is limited to direct bitcoin investments (no GBTC suggestions). We're not even going to get into murky territory like "doing an ICO" or "trying out that crypto loan programme."

THINGS TO THINK ABOUT BEFORE INVESTING IN CRYPTOCURRENCIES

First and foremost, consider the following before investing in cryptocurrency:

1. Complete your homework.

Use exchanges and wallets you're familiar with (I recommend starting with Coinbase/Coinbase Pro; it's arguably the most beginner-friendly exchange/wallet solution). Concentrate on coins you believe in and don't mind "bag holding" (I only recommend Bitcoin and Ethereum; alts are higher risk / higher potential reward). TIP: I would recommend "diversify," but it could be risky for a new investor. Diversify only after you've determined what you're doing. Begin with the safest options, such as Bitcoin (and, to a lesser extent, Ethereum), and work your way down the list to the top alts, such as LTC and XRP.

2. Educate yourself on the history of the market.

Cryptocurrency markets are open 24 hours a day, 7 days a week. Major price movements are common early in the morning when volume is low. Crypto swings up 400% at times, down 80% at others, and sometimes a coin does nothing for months... You'll have a difficult time predicting which of those events will occur next. If you come in during a period when things are going well, you might think things will always be this way, but that has never been the case. Sometimes BTC is up and alts are down, sometimes alts appear to be dominant, sometimes everything is up and down, and so on. Of course, not everything will be up all the time, but when it is, it will not last long (and the mood may change while you are sleeping or out on the weekend on a Saturday night). Only research and/or experience can prepare you for the numerous Bitcoin worlds that exist.

3. Recognize that the market is volatile and that, while investing in cryptocurrencies is legal, many of the risks you will face are significant... Some may even appear to be gambling (similar to penny stock investing; it is investing, but you must be willing to lose up to 100% of your investment if you HODL).

4. Exercise caution and conservatism. By keeping your investment affordable and gradually entering the market over time, you can alleviate a lot of the stress of day-to-day life. A reasonable strategy is to limit your crypto investments to 1%–4% of your investable cash, with buy-ins no more than 10% of

that. Even better if you use stop losses to reduce risk and technical analysis to help you time your trades.

5. Maintain a long-term market perspective. Try not to get too caught up in the present unless your approach requires it. Instead, pick a strategy and an investment, stick to it and keep a long-term view of the market. It's okay to change your strategy in the middle as you gain experience; just make sure you have a plan and a goal in mind. You'll either invest, trade, or do both. If you're investing, try to limit your trading and avoid obsessing over the day's dollar values. Keep an eye on your dollar values if you're trading, and avoid HODLing at the peak.

6. Be aware of your emotions. Your emotions will almost always cost you money. The only time you get lucky and FOMO buy at the bottom or panic sell at the top is when you are lucky. Always rely on data and never on your gut, heart, or anything else that is not based on data. Fear of missing out (FOMO) is a big no-no.

7. Start small. Begin with a small amount of money and gradually increase it once you've determined that everything is working properly. This guidance applies to, among other things, sending money between exchanges, testing a bot or TA approach, trading, and sending money between peers.

8. Be aware of the tax implications and rules. There are a few regulations in place, as well as complex tax rules. Nothing is impossible if you plan ahead of time, but nothing should be overlooked either. As a general rule, if something is controversial in everyday life (online gambling, purchasing items on the dark web, failing to pay your taxes, etc.), it is at the very least suspect in the cryptosphere.

9. Identify the current trend. You'll fare much better if you can tell the difference between a bull and a bear market.

THE BASICS OF INVESTING IN CRYPTOCURRENCIES

If you keep all of the above in mind and intend to invest in or trade cryptocurrencies that interest you, have a good understanding of the market's volatility history, and know which exchanges to use... Then it's time to implement one or two investing/trading strategies (this is preferable to investing everything at once without a clear plan for exiting the market).

Here are some general investing methods that you might be interested in.

Today, go all-in and "just HODL" (try to avoid this one): The simplest thing to do today is to go all-in and "just HODL."

The problem with that method is that it is akin to going up to a roulette table and betting everything on black. While this is correct, the strategy lacks complexity. If you miss the market's absolute bottom, you may find yourself watching your on-paper wealth vanish with few options other than cutting losses or waiting.

Bottom line: Long-term investing is probably the smartest strategy on the planet... until it isn't.

When making an investment, you should always have an exit strategy in place. When a bull market comes to an end, it's usually a good idea to sell or take profits. However, if you're looking for a long-term investment, buy and hold is a viable option, and any price is generally acceptable. Nonetheless, there is a risk of going all in at the top and HODLing the rest of the way down. That can be quite painful, so consider your alternatives.

Before HODLing, take an average position: This is a simple and conservative method that frees you from the shackles of daily price fluctuations. You can either buy at regular intervals regardless of price, or you can buy in increments as the price falls over time. Avoiding market mistiming by accumulating a large position over months or even years is a good way to do so. Meanwhile, as gains appear here and there, you can seize some or all of them (and then reinvest them later if and when more attractive prices appear). It's also possible that one would prefer to gradually transition out of roles. You can reduce your investment risk by gradually joining and exiting positions over time. This is an excellent strategy for a volatile, high-risk, high-reward asset such as Bitcoin. As an added bonus, you may end up paying long-term capital gains tax rather than short-term capital gains tax (which is roughly half as much), and you'll avoid some of the issues that traders face when filing complex crypto taxes.

In conclusion: Averaging in and HODLing is the best bet for new investors. Unquestionably. There is no competition. It's similar to "going all-in and HODLing," but it gives you a lot more breathing room and options for what to do if the market turns against you. Sure, starting this right before a spectacular run isn't as much fun, but in those cases, simply be content with the purchases you made prior to the run. You'll most likely get a chance to buy low soon, and you'll be ready! In some cases, being conservative means exercising caution in exchange for a lower short-term benefit. It's a good trade-off 9 times out of 10.

You don't need to know much more than how to buy and sell cryptocurrency to trade buy low and sell high. Buy at what you believe are low prices, such as the price after a few days of declining prices, and then sell when prices rise. If you make a mistake, you can either set stop losses or "hold bags" (basically reverting to a "build an average position and hold" method). You'll need to learn technical analysis if you want to be a pro at this (TA). TA can be used to make buy and sell decisions based on support and resistance levels, moving averages, and other indicators. If you get it right, TA can help you increase the profitability of your trades, but if you get it wrong, it can demoralise you. Keep an eye on fees and portfolio erosion if you decide to trade. In sideways markets, experienced traders can outperform HODLers, and in down markets, they may outperform them (due to a trader being more apt to sell and wait in cash).

Traders (particularly novice traders) are likely to miss out on some short and dramatic runs as they chase the last coin that performed well into the ground while missing out on the next one in line. If you don't have the time or attention to devote to the volatile crypto markets 24 hours a day, seven days a week, consider trading only a portion of your total investable cash. It takes time and discipline to become a competent crypto trader (super fun, though).

Bottom line: Trading is a fun way to make money if you are skilled, disciplined, and knowledgeable about technical analysis. Trading "noobs" are likely to get "rekt" for a variety of complex reasons.

No one expects a trader to outperform a HODLer, but the majority does (as far as my research suggests). It's okay to get a few bruises on the way to recovery, but don't delude yourself into thinking you've arrived when you haven't. Because you most likely aren't, start with small buyins and don't trade too frequently.

TIP: You can trade cryptocurrency to cryptocurrency or cryptocurrency to cryptocurrency.

Crypto-to-crypto transactions have the added benefit of keeping you in crypto as you try to increase your holdings in a specific coin. It is, however, more difficult than it appears and may cause you to miss out on runs... so keep that in mind.

Purchase a Trading Bot: Trading bots are automated computer programmes that handle your trading for you. The main benefit is that it can carry out your commands while you sleep. It removes all of the stress associated with sleeping. If you plan on trading, it's probably worth your time, effort, and money to set up and manage a bot. You don't have to do anything; simply let it place stop losses for you, or if you know some basic TA, let it trade death crosses and golden crosses on 2hr+ candles (this strategy is common enough that you should be aware of it on any timeframe; if everyone automates it with no additional parameters... every cross will be even more eventful than it is now).

Bottom line: A trading bot may be too demanding for a novice trader who isn't also an amateur coder with some basic trading and TA knowledge (it's not a high bar, but there are some hurdles and learning curves). Once you've mastered the technique, it will take a significant amount of stress out of your day. If the market is falling, you might not be able to sell at 4 a.m. You may not be sitting next to your computer, ready to purchase the Golden Cross that appears while you're at work... but your bot is... and it makes decisions based solely on facts. By removing your emotions, you can allow your crypto-bot to make rational decisions for you.

NOTE: For a TA technique, I mentioned MACD crossings above because short-term averages MUST cross over long-term averages when the price rises and vice versa when the price falls. Other technical indicators are more predictive and help define probability. MACD crosses, on the other hand, are merely a necessary occurrence (which makes them well suited to longer time frame bots focused on investing rather than day trading).

Following the MACD on Bitcoin can give you a good idea of the market's trend.

Invest in a Trading Bot: The term "trading bot" is misleading. When you use a trading bot, you don't have to trade actively. It can be used to build a coin collection or to manage risk (by setting stop losses and stop buys, or by exiting positions only when the charts are very bearish and then reentering as soon as they turn around). You can use a bot to protect or grow your money by employing conservative low-risk/low-reward strategies. You may know you want to invest in Bitcoin, but that doesn't mean you want to sit through an 80% drop. Your emotions may get in the way, but your bot does not, so tell it what you want and then walk away. Finally, if you're going to use a bot, start with this approach. It's a great option for intermediate investors who want to get into cryptocurrency but don't want to be a martyr and HODL every coin they own regardless of market conditions.

Arbitrage: Did you know that you can buy a coin on one exchange for a lower price and sell it for a higher price on another? This is referred to as performing arbitrage between exchanges (or simply "arbitrage"). Arbitrage can be very profitable, but you must act quickly. You can use a bot, but you'll have to grant it withdrawal authority, which can be a pain.

Bottom line: Due to the time it takes to transport cryptos between exchanges, this is a deceptively risky manoeuvre full of traps. When everything is working properly, however, it is very simple and profitable. It's not for inexperienced users, but it's something to strive for in your toolbox. Here's a pro tip: if you already have the coin you're trading into and out of on both exchanges, you can buy and sell right away and then shift the coins (rather than buying, sending, waiting, and selling).

Make a Combination of the Following: A combination of the above can be used to stay safe while learning about and enjoying everything bitcoin has to offer. You can, for example, run one instance of your bot in invest mode and another in trading mode, trade a little manually, and keep the rest of your funds in a secure offline wallet. On the other hand, maybe your bank account outweighs all of your good intentions, and your bots protect you from emotional trading? The issue is that if one thing performs exceptionally well for you while the others do not, you now know what type of investor/trader you should be.

Bottom line: This is difficult because it requires learning and applying various solutions. This, on the other hand, should and would be the ultimate goal for the vast majority of people. So why not use them in tandem, selecting the appropriate tool for each job if you have sufficient mastery of each tool to use it?

TA STRATEGIC OPTIONS: When it comes to TA, it's critical to stick to the basics until you've figured out "what is the best TA-based investing strategy for me?"

For example, I like to look for bullish and bearish crossovers using MACD and GUPPY moving averages (because they can't go wrong; they must cross over if the market is bullish and under if it's bearish). However, you should work on honing your style. Similarly, I prefer to stop and ladder into and out of currencies with small buy-ins, always keeping some cash and the rest in crypto, but I can't tell you how to play your hand. Again, I'm attempting to provide general strategies rather than specifics in this section.

ALTCOIN INVESTMENT STRATEGIES YOU SHOULD BE AWARE OF

1. Before leaping, take a deep breath.

You cannot enter any trade or investment arena, whether stocks or altcoins, unless you first thoroughly understand the market and the currencies in which you wish to invest.

Crypto markets are more volatile than traditional stock markets, which are mediated by regulatory organisations such as the SEBI in India and deal in pegged financial assets 24 hours a day, seven days a week. As a result, you should be aware that cryptocurrency markets are prone to rapid mood swings.

Keeping track of the market's history or the performance of a specific cryptocurrency, investor sentiment, current developments in the crypto ecosystem, bearish or bullish market patterns, and other factors will assist you in understanding the situation.

You don't have to empty your altcoin wallet every time the price of a cryptocurrency rises or falls. Instead, go for the currencies you believe in, read their whitepaper, look at their team and roadmap, and examine the technology they use to boost your confidence.

Following that, having a well-defined investment strategy with a clear goal will help you get through even the most difficult times. Finally, think about how long you want to hold the currency: minutes, hours, days, months, or even years. Alternatively, you can decide whether you want to day trade altcoins or 'bag hold' them for the long term.

Use a reputable cryptocurrency exchange to trade or deal in altcoins. WazirX, India's most renowned cryptocurrency exchange, for example, enables you to trade securely, quickly, and conveniently.

2. Don't put all of your eggs in a single basket.

The crypto world is a volatile place where events like a minor technical team spat in Tezos or Musk yelling 'DOGE, DOGE, BABY DOGE' on Twitter can either shatter or build markets. As a result, investing in a single currency is risky. Rather, diversify your portfolio by investing in a variety of altcoins. The top ten cryptocurrencies by market capitalization,

149

excluding Bitcoin, such as Dash, ETH, XRP, Litecoin, Cardano, and others, would be the safest bet for newcomers.

Extra altcoin investment advice: Invest in cryptocurrencies that have not yet reached their full growth potential to see your investment multiply several times over time as the altcoin gains popularity.

Sign up for #mc embed

/ * background:#fff; clear:left; font:14px Helvetica,Arial,sansserif; Add your own Mailchimp form style overrides to your site's CSS or this style block. This block, as well as the preceding CSS link, should be moved to the HEAD of your HTML file.

(function($)window.fnames = new Array(); window.ftypes = new Array();fnames[0]='EMAIL';ftypes[0]='email'; (jQuery));var $mcj = jQuery.noConflict(true); 3 Put your trust in the fundamentals.

3. Unlike traditional equities, altcoins are far more than just financial instruments that can be traded. They each have their own set of concrete goals. Some, such as smart contract platforms Ethereum or NEO, or decentralized storage networks Filecoin or Storj, aid in the mediation of currency prices, others in the acceleration of payment processes, and still others in the strengthening of a platform's transparency and accountability. Rather than relying on public opinion, evaluate the coin's fundamentals using this two-pronged approach:

To estimate the altcoin's lifespan, consider its viability, practical application, and scope.

Examine the scope and impact of the company's upcoming partnerships and releases on its market performance.

To reduce risk, diversify your altcoin portfolio within the category rather than investing in coins from different 'categories.'

4. Keep Emotions at Bay and Concentrate on the Technical

FOMO, or any other gut, liver, or heart emotion, is not supported by numbered evidence. You can, however, multiply your cryptocurrency investments by learning the intricacies of technical analysis. Simply determine whether the price is rising or falling, fluctuating or remaining constant, and adjust your investment strategy accordingly. If you know the 50-day SMA (Simple Moving Average) for a particular altcoin, for example, you can identify positive price swings once the altcoin's price begins to move above its SMA.

The ATH (All-Time High) price of an altcoin is another important technical indicator. You can calculate what proportion of the altcoin's ATH value corresponds to its current price.

If you study these signs before trading on a regular basis, you will be able to make more informed trading decisions.

5. Should I HODL, Stake, or Mine?

There are numerous ways to grow your crypto investments depending on the altcoin you've invested in:

Cryptocurrency is the safest, simplest, and quickest way to generate passive income from your assets. To invest in altcoins, all you need is a secure crypto wallet and a reputable

151

exchange. Furthermore, you can buy cryptocurrencies in small increments and gradually increase your holdings.

Staking is a method of generating passive income from your cryptocurrency investment by freezing or staking it on a network and earning interest.

Mining altcoins can also provide you with monthly dividends.

Individuals interested in earning rewards through mining should consider cloud mining or joining a mining pool, as solo mining is costly and time-consuming, particularly in the case of Bitcoin.

6. Safeguard Your Cryptocurrency Investments

To hedge your crypto assets, you must play the diversification game wisely. So, what is the best way to go about it? Think outside the box to diversify your assets beyond cryptos in stocks, gold, and other traditional instruments to create a market-spanning portfolio. A portfolio that includes both equities and cryptos can help you overcome the high correlation of the crypto market. Simply put, an upward trend in Bitcoin, which accounts for 45 percent of the crypto market, always leads to an upward trend in the rest of the crypto market, and vice versa. As a result, in the event of a market crash, there are no safe crypto assets' on which to rely. As a result, it's no surprise that large investment funds are attempting to combine the two these days.

7. Begin small and work your way up to liquidity.

Have a practise run before you go all-in on the crypto market. Begin with small investments and gradually increase the size of your portfolio over time. Once you realise you're on the right track, there's no turning back. Trading on a regular basis is another simple way to keep your money moving and multiplying.

Liquidity is essential for the safety and fluidity of crypto investments. Altcoins with low trading volumes are frequently chosen by investors. This choice may turn out to be a disadvantage. Although the price of altcoins may rise several times, you cannot profit from selling them. Even if you are able to sell a large number of coins, prices may fall due to a lack of liquidity. So, how do you keep yourself safe? Cryptocurrencies with low volume should be avoided at all costs!

CHAPTER 10
TEN BUSINESS MODELS IN THE METAVERSE

What is it about the Metaverse that draws people in?

From a technical standpoint, blockchain grants enforceable property rights to all digital assets. 3D and multimedia have long been the dominant trends in Internet development. From text communications to photos, videos, and live broadcasts, the Internet has evolved in a more vivid direction. Metaverse combines two perspectives: it is based on blockchain technology and adheres to the rich content trend. So, what kind of business models will exist in the future Metaverse?

The sale of NFTs

Galleries are now the most popular business model in Metaverse, which may be due to the internal relationship between NFT and art. Many of the original Metaverse participants were painters or worked in the arts. CryptoVoxels' works in the Korean community include Liu Jiaying's "Pure Gold Gallery," Song Ting's "Panda Gallery," BCA Gallery, and the Doge Sound Club. This is the first and most popular business model for Metaverse.

Sales of voxes

Unlike the real world, the Metaverse is made up of various materials. For example, in CryptoVoxels, all structures and wearable devices are made entirely of voxels, which are digital values on a three-dimensional grid. As a result, in CryptoVoxels, the use of vox is required, and it serves as an architectural ornament or personal display.

Many vox stores have sprung up on the scene to meet this demand, with voxWalk being the most visible example of the business concept.

In the metaverse, there are ten business models.

In the future, your company may need to purchase virtual billboards, interact with fans on platforms like Discord, and

155

collaborate with firms like Jadu or The Fabricant to create virtual assets. They will act as a bridge between traditional businesses and augmented and virtual reality.

Metaverse will develop sophisticated and innovative advertising campaigns that blur the distinction between the physical and virtual worlds.

Construction

Some landowners have a lot of plots but don't have the time or energy to build them. Other landowners use expert teams to build their plots in order to develop their brand. As a result of this demand, third-party construction services such as MetaEstate and Voxel Architects have grown in the Metaverse. Voxel Architects designed the top four structures with the most visitors on CryptoVoxels' main island, Origin City: SpaceAge, StoneAge, GlassAge, and Welcome.

MetaEstate also built well-known and aesthetically pleasing structures such as the MetaChi headquarters and the Creation Fashion Hub.

Lease of digital parcels

Digital packages, like physical real estate, can be leased and purchased. According to CV Analytics' findings, many landowners own multiple plots. Most landowners do not intend to build on their plots, preferring to invest in them for the long term. As a result, a natural land lease market has emerged, allowing landowners to lease their unused property to others in need of development or operation.

Experiential learning

People who are overly focused on creating the atmosphere and have lost sight of reality are immersed.

At Universal Studios Beijing, when Harry Potter raises the moving chair, hops atop the tower with Transformers, and the minion Fiddle around together, the ostensibly tangible experience is a kind of spiritual immersion. As a result, Metaverse is a natural environment based on expert architectural design and an immersive 3D experience.

Game

Because of their virtual nature, games are simple to integrate into the Metaverse. The Sandbox is a blockchain game platform that allows developers to convert voxel assets and in-game gadgets into NFTs. Of course, games can be integrated into other Metaverse platforms. Participating in on-chain games allows players to have fun while investing in NFT.

Clothes sales

In some ways, the Metaverse will never be able to replace the real world. Clothing, food, shelter, and transportation, for example, are all basic material needs. Online clothing sales, in particular, have progressed from the introduction of 2D images in the past to live try-on and are now moving toward 3D in the future. In reality, watching others try on clothes has a different effect than trying on one's own. For example, you could use a 3D scanner to place your 3D virtual version of clothes on your 3D virtual version.

KTV on the internet

For those who enjoy it, KTV is a form of socialising. It's difficult for people who live far apart to meet in KTV in the real world. However, in the Metaverse, these wishes may come true.

service for data

The Metaverse is no exception to the fact that data is all around us. For example, the platform necessitates visitor data for each package, potential buyers necessitate historical data on the package sold, and potential sellers necessitate market data to determine their asking price. Each of the preceding requires data assistance, and a skilled data analysis provider could become a profitable business.

There are ten different business models in the Metaverse.

There could be a lot of new jobs available soon. Examples include Metaverse architects, Metaverse game planners, construction and operation professionals, and so on. In addition to the ten listed above, there are undoubtedly other successful business concepts.

So, what does the future of the Metaverse hold? A three-dimensional "Twitter," combining social media and advertising? An immersive project experience, one after the other? Is there a market for 3D fittings and fittings on the internet? Is it possible to have a global karaoke KTV? These are not, just as Facebook, Google, and Amazon cannot represent the Internet on their own; rather, they must connect and interact with other platforms in order to create a true Metaverse.

In the Metaverse, blockchain enables enterprise business models.

158

Enterprise blockchain has come a long way since its inception in 2017. Originally, blockchain for business was a system based on private, permissioned networks that were primarily used for the supply chain management. As blockchain matured, businesses began to use public, permissionless networks like Ethereum to conduct business.

Businesses in the Metaverse are implementing decentralized concepts to develop more efficient procedures in 2021. While describing the Metaverse is difficult, William Herkelrath, head of business development at Chainlink Labs, a decentralized oracle network, told Cointelegraph that he believes it is a collection of ecosystems that are naturally arising from decentralized finance or Defi:

"Because they must interact with the outside world, businesses will be required to establish ecosystems in the Metaverse." Consumers, for example, want to use loyalty programmes that are not limited to a single platform, so they will choose brands that provide incentives that can be used across multiple ecosystems. Furthermore, in the Metaverse, data, physical assets, commercial, and financial assets can all be built up in a layer separate from a centralised system." "

The Enterprise Metaverse

While the concept may appear far-fetched, an increasing number of blockchain-based businesses are beginning to embrace the Metaverse. This topic was discussed in depth at the European Blockchain Convention's virtual conference last Wednesday during a panel titled "Building the Enterprise Multiverse."

David Palmer, the blockchain lead at Vodafone Business, stated during the conversation that the Metaverse is much more than a virtual environment where digital experiences can be had through games or social media networks. The Metaverse, according to Palmer, is now being used to apply blockchain technology to financial concepts such as central bank digital currencies, nonfungible tokens, NFTs, and Defi.

Palmer, on the other hand, pointed out that the Metaverse lacks a layer that allows virtual transactions to be transferred to the real world. According to Palmer, a cell phone can act as a bridge between these two worlds. Vodafone Business is using blockchain to create digital identities that can be used in both the Metaverse and in real life, he told Cointelegraph. "Digital identification will bridge the gap between the digital and physical worlds," he said. A digital wallet, for example, will include a bank account, mortgage information, tokens, and NFTs. In contrast, a decentralized identity will have access to those credentials, allowing people to participate in both the Metaverse and the real world." "

Palmer revealed that Vodafone Business is working on mobile device virtual identity wallets. Furthermore, Greyscale Research discussed the concept of self-sovereign identity in a multiverse in a recent study titled "The Metaverse, Web 3.0 Virtual Cloud Economies." The study describes selfsovereign identification as a "internet-native social reputation coin (creator coins)," mentioning that data from other platforms can be imported into the Metaverse and used for identity or credit score.

Angel Garcia, Telefonica's head of global supply chain strategy and transformation, described how a digital supply chain for the Metaverse could help telcos become more efficient during the discussion. According to Garcia, Telefonica has developed a blockchain network that will be used within the Metaverse ecosystem. He went on to say that the company is actively collecting data in order to optimise end-to-end operations. "The next stage will be to automate and centralise those business operations for everyone," he said.

According to Rowan Fenn, co-founder of rising X, an enterprise solution for companies looking to build autonomous digital organisations, businesses can have a digital twin of their autonomous organisation to govern, operate, and control analogue processes: "In a Multiverse, these organisations will be able to interact and transact with one another in realtime." The autonomous digital groups will be able to collaborate as a result of this." "

According to Fenn, companies with a digital twin in a Multiverse ecosystem will be able to generate more goods and services while using fewer resources. As a result, he believes that by employing this business model, the world will be able to transition from a finite to an unlimited economy.

Blockchain is already being used by businesses in the Metaverse.

While businesses investigate early use cases for implementing business models in the Metaverse, certain industries have already begun to do so. According to Herkelrath, the use of blockchain networks in the insurance industry, for example, exemplifies a Metaverse business model.

According to Herkelrath, virtual ecosystems are selling hundreds of thousands of insurance contracts to farmers all over the world. He went on to say that smart contracts built on top of blockchain networks, as well as decentralized oracles like Chainlink, have enabled the insurance industry to overcome its transparency issues. Furthermore, the entire insurance procedure has been streamlined so that alienated clients can access it from anywhere in the world.

Although it may appear that blockchain alone is responsible for this, Herkelrath points out that smart contracts created by insurance companies require data that cannot be obtained without the Metaverse:

"You have a metaverse of companies with data flowing in that is confirmed by a larger network, making this feasible." The fact that this can occur in the Metaverse demonstrates that business-to-consumer transactions can become affordable and accessible to anyone, anywhere. "

What is the likelihood that businesses will embrace the Metaverse?

While some businesses are developing and implementing Metaverse business models, a lack of understanding of the technology may stymie adoption. During the panel discussion, Rodolfo Quijano, the head of a blockchain at Henkel, a German chemical and consumer goods company, stated that the main issue driving adoption now is recognising the value that the Metaverse can provide to businesses: "Technology isn't an issue; however, people will need more time to understand what blockchain is and how it compares to traditional enterprise resource planning tools." It can be difficult to find champions for blockchain adoption in the Metaverse." "

"The most important aspect for a teleco to address is how to connect individuals in the Metaverse," Palmer said, adding that scalability within a Metaverse enterprise setting is also a concern, as is getting organisations to understand how to transition and participate in this new technology. Furthermore, people will have two identities, one virtual and one real, raising the question of whether we will have enough communication bandwidth." "

Furthermore, Palmer believes that firms will question the function of blockchain when it comes to Metaverse business models. However, he believes that technology is essential for these applications. "Blockchain serves as the trust and exchange layer in a multiverse. It's a massive opportunity, but corporations will find it difficult to adapt." "

IN THE METAVERSE, MARKETING

Digital marketers must keep up with technological advancements. Understanding the metaverse and its full potential is one aspect of this. Marketers must understand that the metaverse isn't a passing fad; it appears to be here to stay and poised to become the next big thing.

What strategies might marketers use as the metaverse grows?

Marketers must remember, first and foremost, the importance of millennials and Gen Zers as a target audience.

These generations are also interested in metaverses, such as Roblox games and virtual reality technologies.

With that in mind, let's take a look at how to market in the metaverse.

There is parallel metaverse marketing within real-life marketing.

Create marketing experiences that are related to real-life events or are similar to what your company currently does. In June, for example, AB InBev's Stella Artois collaborated with Zed Run to create a Tamagotchi-themed Kentucky Derby experience. They did so because AB InBev's Stella Artois is well-known for its support of sports, particularly horse racing. As a result, it appears that developing an online platform where non-fungible token (NFT) horses can be sold, raced, and produced is the next logical step for them.

Immersive experience is essential.

In the metaverse, you can sell virtual advertising. Bidstack, a video game ad tech company, for example, has shifted away from the traditional outdoor advertising and toward virtual billboard advertising.

However, virtual billboards aren't the only option.

Because metaverses are naturally fascinating and immersive, it's a good idea to capitalise on this by providing a comparable immersive experience in your advertisements and marketing efforts. Instead of simply displaying advertisements, provide branded installations and events with which users can interact.

Immersive experiences have been provided to consumers by early adopters, such as a Lil Nas X performance in Roblox, Gucci Garden experience visits, and Warner Bros.' marketing of In the Heights with a virtual recreation of the Washington Heights area. Brands have also recently discovered new revenue streams through collaborations with the Roblox metaverse and other metaverses.

There should be collectibles available.

People enjoy collecting things, and the metaverse provides them with yet another outlet to do so. You can replicate the experience in the metaverse by providing assets or limited-edition items that can only be obtained in the metaverse.

The Collector's Room, for example, can be found in the Gucci Garden Roblox experience. It enables users to amass limited-edition Gucci items in the metaverse. Gucci earned a total of 286,000,000 Robux from the game's initial collectible product sales.

Take part in existing communities.

The general public despises advertising. As a result, it's critical for businesses looking to enter the metaverse to avoid offending people who are already there. You'll need their positive feedback because you'll be marketing to them.

It's critical to remember that you can't just jump on a new platform without thinking about the new format.

Businesses gain traction when they collaborate with members of the Roblox developer community, for example, to create goods and experiences. Similarly, when O2 produced a

Fortnite show, they enlisted the assistance of coders who were already familiar with the game.

This is an illustration of influencer marketing. Because user-generated content is so important, community members play a critical role in the success of your campaigns.

Experiment all the time.

Marketers are living in an exciting time. While some guidelines can help marketers decide which approaches and methods to use, the metaverse is still a young platform with plenty of room for experimentation. Best practises are still being established, and paradigms are being developed as a whole.

Marketers have a lot of leeway to try new things and be creative in their tactics as a result of this.

Other Surprising Metaverse Cases

• Dimension Studio's metaverse experimenting for fashion companies brought in $6.5 million.

They created a virtual production setup in which customers can walk onto a platform, have their bodies scanned by 106 cameras, and then be placed in virtual worlds to try on garments and other items.

They are well-known for their work on Balenciaga's Autumn/Winter 2021 Afterworld game.

• Grand Theft Auto V, an open-world sandbox game, included outfit options similar to those worn by Hong Kong demonstrators. Many artists have used virtual worlds to express themselves politically, and demonstrators in Hong Kong may be able to take their fight beyond the physical world and into the metaverse.

• On Houzz, a home decor website, users can create digital photo collections of their furniture and other household items. Every time someone buys something on Houzz, they make money. In 2017, they developed a 3D viewer that allows customers to see products in 3D directly through a camera, visually integrating them into their actual environment. • Google Maps demonstrated an augmented reality application for its walking directions. This feature allows users to get precise visual directions and arrows to help them get to their destinations. Simply point the user's camera in the direction they need to go, and the AR feature will send them there.

CHAPTER 11

PROFITING FROM THE METAVERSE

For a long time, virtual places and worlds have been popular. Through games like Sims City and the GTA series, people become immersed in virtual environments. Because these games became a worldwide sensation, virtual worlds, also known as 'MetaVerse,' have been a successful addition to future technology.

Metaverses have advanced to the point where people see this technology as economically beneficial to the planet. Unfortunately, prior to incorporating this worldview, metaverses were virtual tools with no reality-based reference.

168

Another area that has had a significant impact on market conditions is cryptocurrency and blockchain. Because of the widespread adoption of blockchain, the market has been presented with actual and industrial-based solutions. As a result, it is expected that digital-based technology will take over the role of providing monetary-based solutions to the rest of the world.

The Metaverse is, in fact, based on science fiction. It is formed by two prefixes: "meta" for "beyond" and "verse" for "universe." The Metaverse is the end result of all the internet-enabled virtual worlds that have been created. Using augmented reality and virtual reality, avatars that communicate virtually and have digital assets that are end-to-end blockchain encrypted have been created. It's a virtual-reality environment in which people interact with one another in a setting that is generated automatically.

Although metaverses have existed for some time, the underlying technology has yet to bring permissionless identities, financial services, or high-speed exchanges to the general market. Instead, cryptocurrencies and blockchain created a system for sharing and storing billions of people's data in order to create a reality-based link between the virtual and real worlds.

Metaverses' entire concept of operation changed dramatically as they became more focused on incorporating blockchain technology as an 'engine' for these platforms. Metaverses have always had a financial system because they are virtual worlds. These in-game currencies had no value before blockchain became a part of the virtual world because they lacked a physical form. The concept of 'Decentralization' influenced the platforms soon after blockchain was integrated into the Metaverse phenomenon. Blockchain-based platforms had their own NFTs and cryptocurrency, which were used to create, own, and monetize virtual assets.

One of the technological breakthroughs was the ability to establish genuine worth by allowing the sale of NFTs into real cash via the Metaverse's dedicated NFT marketplaces. Axie Infinity, Decentraland, and SecondLive are examples of commercially successful virtual worlds that allow users to make a fortune by participating in them.

WHAT IS THE MOST EFFECTIVE WAY TO INVEST IN METAVERSES?

As metaverses were normalised as a system that runs over the blockchain, people were introduced to various types of entries. As a result, depending on how the virtual world operates, investors can invest in both active and passive ways.

The user was actively involved in the game and the virtual environment. Metaverses, as a complete world, had a plethora of categories, each with its own set of applications. A player who plays the game and is a part of the Metaverse earns money and NFT tokens (that the Metaverse runs on). These accumulated tokens are valuable in the financial world and can be traded on any metaverse marketplace. Furthermore, users can exchange their tokens for major cryptocurrencies.

Users can invest in the Metaverse passively while focusing on the active investing style. In the crypto world, the NFT coin, which is used throughout the Metaverse, or NFT Metaverse, has monetary value. As the project grows in size, it will be able to list itself on various exchanges and platforms. Furthermore, because it is a part of several IDOs and launchpads, investors can pool their money across the exchange or platform to profit. This marks the end of passive investor participation in the Metaverse.

Investors' exposure to Metaverses through the purchase of a Metaverse ETF is another recognised strategy for investing in Metaverses. An exchange-traded fund (ETF) is a pool of securities and safeties that trade on a stock exchange like stocks. A metaverse stock ETF allows investors to invest in companies that already have a strong position in the crypto ecosystem.

METAVERSE CAN HELP YOU MAKE MONEY IN WHAT WAYS?

Being a part of the game is one of the most understandable explanations for how to make money in the Metaverse offered by the user. Because these metaverses use the 'Play-to-Earn' method, you can make a lot of money just by playing the game.

Passive investment is yet another way to profit from metaverses. Before investing, people are advised to do their homework on a project. Discovering the project's outstanding use cases and road map will undoubtedly provide you with significant benefits in a short period of time.

The Metaverse is advancing tenfold in terms of technology.

There is a lot to show because these systems are limitless, capable of performing a wide range of functions in the virtual world. Many use cases can be implemented because we all agree that the scope of metaverses is infinite. You should improve your conceptual understanding if you want to profit from the metaverse. As a result, more concepts and distinctiveness will eventually be included in metaverses. Investing in technology on your own would assist you in making it extremely profitable.

The Metaverse and virtual worlds have presented a logical strategy for connecting the digital and physical worlds.

One of the most notable factors that arrived to definitively branch the link was blockchain. Furthermore, the metaverse provides users with a plethora of options and greatly benefits from the system.

CHAPTER 12

A STEP-BY-STEP GUIDE TO PURCHASING REAL ESTATE IN THE METAVERSE

Metaverse is a step toward digitising the real world by combining augmented reality (AR), virtual reality (VR), and video. Users can use their digital avatars to work, play, and communicate with friends in the virtual world. There are numerous activities available in the metaverse, ranging from organising a meeting to taking a virtual globe tour.

Real estate, on the other hand, appears to be capturing the attention of investors. The volume of property deals in the metaverse has been making headlines, with unprecedented million-dollar purchases reported every other week.

To buy virtual property, you must first sign up for a metaverse platform like Decentraland, The Sandbox, or Axie Infinity, among others. Then, all you need to transact in the metaverse is a well-funded digital wallet. Then, you can keep your dollars in your digital wallet by converting them to cryptocurrencies like ether or native currencies of the metaverse in which you're transacting, such as MANA or Sandbox.

With the help of the metaverse's nearly complete ecosystem, you can buy, rent, flip, or even sell homes in the digital world, and ownership is based on non-fungible tokens (NFTs).

173

The steps below will walk you through the process of purchasing real estate in the metaverse.

1. Log in to one of the metaverse's real estates marketplaces, such as Decentraland, Axie Infinity, or Sandbox.

2. Compare the prices of the various available parcels of land.

3. Once you've decided on the digital plot of land you'd like to purchase, click on it to learn more about it. It's important to remember that a particular metaverse property platform will only allow you to buy from them if you use their approved cryptocurrency. For example, Decentraland only allows users to buy and sell homes using MANA, the company's cryptocurrency.

4. The next step is to link your digital wallet to your property site account. To do so, you must first acquire a suitable digital wallet. Right now, Metamask is the most popular digital wallet on the market. Furthermore, it is compatible with almost every metaverse property platform.

5. You must fund your digital wallet with a cryptocurrency that is compatible with the digital property platform you have chosen. Then, you can easily purchase it on various exchanges and store the cryptos in your digital wallet. When you've finished selecting the land and funding your associated digital wallet, all you have to do is press the 'purchase' button.

6. Once the transaction is completed, the digital land you purchased is saved as NFTs in your associated digital wallet. So, in your digital wallet, navigate to the 'NFTs' tab to see your newly purchased land.

What you should know before purchasing metaverse property

In contrast to investing in the real estate market, where your purchased physical land is guaranteed to survive, digital land in the metaverse will become non-existent if the platform you purchased fails and shuts down. Another consideration is the high volatility of the cryptocurrency used to transact in the metaverse's real estate market. Because the value of digital money fluctuates, so does the value of the metaverse property you own.

Furthermore, because digital real estate is a new asset class, many aspects remain unexplored. As a result, investing in the metaverse's digital real estate market is highly speculative; as a result, thoroughly researching the benefits and drawbacks is advised before making any decisions.

CHAPITRE 13

NETWORKING AND THE METAVERSE

For most readers, the three main networking aspects — bandwidth, latency, and dependability — will be the least interesting Metaverse-enablers. However, their limitations and growth have an impact on how we build Metaverse products and services, when we can use them, and what we can (and cannot) accomplish.

Bandwidth

Bandwidth is frequently confused with speed, despite the fact that it refers to the amount of data that can be sent in a given amount of time. The Metaverse's requirements are far more stringent than those of most internet apps and games, as well as many current connections. The best way to understand this is to use Microsoft Flight Simulator.

Microsoft Flight Simulator is the most realistic and largest consumer simulation in history. It includes nearly every road, mountain, city, and airport on the planet, as well as 2 trillion individually rendered trees, 1.5 billion structures, and nearly every road, mountain, city, and airport... They all look like the real thing because they are based on high-quality scans of the original object.'

Microsoft Flight Simulator, on the other hand, requires over 2.5 petabytes of data — or 2,500,000 gigabytes — to accomplish this. This amount of data would not be stored on a consumer device (or most enterprise devices).

Even if they could, Microsoft Flight Simulator is a real-time service that updates to reflect current weather and air traffic (including precise wind speed and direction, temperature, humidity, rain, and lighting). As a result, you can fly into real-world hurricanes and storms while following the same flight path as commercial planes in real life.

Microsoft Flight Simulator works by saving a small amount of data locally on your computer (which, like any console game, also runs the game, as opposed to cloud-based game-streaming services like Stadia). When users are connected to the internet, Microsoft sends massive amounts of data to the local player's device on a need-to-know basis.

Consider it in the same way that you would a real-world pilot.

As they pass over a mountain or around a bend, new light information floods into their retinas, revealing and then clarifying what's there for the first time. After that, all they have is the knowledge that something will be present before then.

Many players believe that all online multiplayer video games operate in this manner. In reality, most game providers only send positional data, player input data (e.g., throw a bomb, shoot), and summary-level data (e.g., players remaining in a battle royale) to individual players. Because all of the asset and rendering data is already on your local device, the download and installation times, as well as the hard disc consumption, are quite lengthy.

By transmitting rendering data as needed, games can have a much wider variety of things, assets, and environments. Furthermore, they can accomplish this without the use of game-delaying downloads and installations, update batching, or massive user hard drives. As a result, many games now employ a hybrid paradigm that blends locally stored data with data streaming. This strategy, on the other hand, is critical for systems that are focused on the Metaverse. Roblox, for example, necessitates (and benefits from) a wider range of assets, items, and environments than Mario Kart or Call of Duty.

As the complexity and importance of virtual simulation grow, so will the amount of data that must be broadcast. For the time being, Roblox benefits from a variety of basic prefabs and assets that have been widely recycled and lightly modified. As a result, Roblox primarily streams information about modifying previously downloaded items. However, the virtual platform will eventually necessitate an almost infinite number of permutations and constructions (nearly all of which it will be unable to predict accurately).

Virtual twinning systems (also known as mirror worlds,' such as Microsoft Flight Simulator) must already mimic the real world's practically infinite (and demonstrable) variability. This requires sending significantly more (i.e., heavier) data than 'dark cloud here' or 'a dark cloud that is 95% similar to dark cloud C-95'. It's actually a dark cloud that looks exactly like this. Most importantly, this information is updated in real time.

The significance of the final point cannot be overstated.
179

If we want to interact in a massive, real-time, shared, and persistent virtual world, we'll need a flood of cloud-streamed data.

(One of these is made up.)

Compare the'real world' to the Fortnite map.

Everyone on the planet is immersed in the same simulation at the same time and in the same location. If I fell a tree, it is irreversibly lost to everyone. When playing Fortnite, you can only see a fixed, point-in-time version of the map. And whatever you do on that map is only shared with a few others and only for a short period of time before being reset. Is it legal to fell a tree? It will be reset in 1–25 minutes, and it has previously only been removed for up to 99 other users. The map is only updated when a new edition of Epic Games is released. And if Epic Games decided to broadcast your universe to the rest of the world, they'd choose your universe, disregard theirs, and place your universe in a specific time period. This is sufficient for many virtual experiences. It will also be adequate for a variety of Metaverse-specific experiences. Some (but not all) experiences, on the other hand, will necessitate consistency across all users and at all times.

Cloud data streaming is also required if we are to move fluidly between virtual worlds. For example, the Travis Scott concert in Fortnite transported players from the game's main area to the depths of a previously unseen ocean, then to a previously unseen planet, and finally far into space. Epic accomplished this by distributing all of these game worlds to players via a standard Fortnite patch days or hours before the event (which, of course, meant that anyone who hadn't downloaded and installed the update prior to the event couldn't participate). During each set piece, the following set-piece was loaded in the background on each player's device. This method works very well, but it requires a publisher to know which worlds a user will visit next and how far in advance they will do so. If you want to choose from a wide range of locations, you must either download the entirety of all available alternatives (which is not possible) or cloud stream them.

Along with the additional environmental data, there is also more player data. When you see your friend in Fortnite today, all the Fortnite server has to do is tell you where they are and what they're up to; the animations (such as reloading an assault rifle or falling) are already loaded onto your device and only need to run. However, when real-time motion capture is mapped to a friend's avatar, this detailed information must be supplied along with the rest of us. If you want to watch a video file within the game, as Fortnite occasionally does, you must do so via a virtual world. Can you hear the spatial audio of a crowd? Same. Have you ever had a passerby brush up against the shoulder of your haptic bodysuit? Same.

Many players are already experiencing bandwidth and network congestion when playing online games that only require positional and input data. These requirements will be amplified by the Metaverse. The good news is that broadband penetration and bandwidth are increasing globally. Compute, which will be discussed further in Section #3, is also improving and can help replace constrained data transfer by forecasting what will happen until real data can be substituted.

Latency

181

The most difficult networking problem is also the most misunderstood: latency. Latency is the amount of time it takes for data to travel from one location to another and back.

When compared to network capacity (above) and dependability, latency is frequently regarded as the least important KPI (below). This is because most internet transmission is one-way or asynchronous. It doesn't matter whether the time between sending a WhatsApp message and receiving a read receipt is 100ms, 200ms, or even two seconds. It also doesn't matter if you press the pause button on YouTube and the video ends in 20ms, 150ms, or 300ms. When watching Netflix, it is more important that the stream continues to play than that it begins immediately. Netflix accomplishes this by delaying the start of a video stream, allowing your device to download ahead of time while you watch. You won't notice if your network hiccups or crunches for a few seconds this way.

Even synchronous and persistent communications, such as video calls, have a relatively high tolerance for latency. Because video is the least important aspect of the calls, video-calling software usually prioritises voice, the 'lightest' data, if the network is congested. And if your latency spikes — even to the point of seconds rather than milliseconds — software can help by speeding up audio-backlog playback and quickly removing pauses. Furthermore, by simply learning to wait a little longer, participants can easily manage latency.

For the most engaging AAA online multiplayer games, low latency is required. This is due to the fact that latency governs how quickly a player receives information (e.g., where they are, whether a grenade has been thrown, or whether a soccer ball has been kicked) and how quickly their response is relayed to other players. In other words, latency determines whether you win or lose, whether you kill or die. This is why, despite our resistance to higher frame rates for traditional video, most modern games run at 2–4 times the usual video framerate, and why we've quickly accepted these increases.

It's a prerequisite for success.

The human latency threshold in video gaming is extremely low, especially when compared to other mediums.

Think about the difference between a regular video and a video game. If audio and video are out of sync by more than 45 milliseconds or 125 milliseconds, the average person will not notice (170ms total). At 90 milliseconds early and 185 milliseconds late, acceptance levels are much higher (275ms). When we don't get a response from a digital button, such as a YouTube stop button, after 200–250ms, we assume our clicks failed. Even nongamers become irritated after 50 milliseconds in AAA games, and nongamers feel disadvantaged after 110 milliseconds. At 150ms, games are unplayable. Subspace claims that a 10ms increase or decrease in latency reduces or increases weekly playtime by 6%. That is a once-in-a-lifetime opportunity available to no other company.

With the above ranges in mind, let's take a look at global average latency. In the United States, the average roundtrip time for data transported from one city to another and back is 35 milliseconds. Many pairings exceed this, especially in densely populated areas with high-demand peaks (for example, San Francisco to New York in the evening). Then there's the 'city-to-user' transit time, which is particularly prone to delays. Cities,

183

communities, and condominiums in densely populated areas can become congested very quickly. If you're using a mobile device, 4G technology adds another 40 milliseconds. Finally, if you live outside of a major metropolitan area, your data may have to travel an additional 100 miles over ancient, poorly maintained wireline infrastructure. The global median delivery latency varies by city and ranges between 100 and 200 milliseconds.

To manage latency, the online gaming industry has devised a number of partial fixes and hacks. However, none of them scale well.

For example, most high-fidelity multiplayer gaming is based on server regions. Limiting the player roster to those in the Northeast United States, Western Europe, or Southeast Asia can help game publishers reduce geographical latency. This clustering works well enough because gaming is a leisure activity that is frequently shared with one to three friends. After all, it's unlikely that you'll be playing with someone who lives in a different time zone. And, in any case, you don't care where your unknown opponents (with whom you can't normally communicate) live.

Nonetheless, according to Subspace, roughly three-quarters of all internet connections in the Middle East are outside of playable latency limits for dynamic multiplayer games, while only a quarter is in the US and Europe.

This is primarily due to limitations in broadband infrastructure rather than server placement.

In multiplayer online games, 'Netcode' solutions are also used to ensure synchronisation and consistency, as well as to keep players engaged. Delay-based netcode instructs a player's device (such as a PlayStation 5) to delay rendering the owner's inputs until the inputs of the more latent player (i.e., their opponent) arrive. This will irritate players with low-latency muscle memory, but it is effective. The netcode for rollback is more sophisticated. If an opponent's inputs are delayed, a player's device will behave as expected. If it is discovered that the opponent did something other than what was expected, the device will attempt to unwind in-progress animations and then 'properly' replay them.

These solutions work well for 1v1 games (e.g., 2D fighters), tiny latency issues (e.g., 40ms), and titles with a narrow range of highly predictable behaviours (e.g., a driving game, a 2D fighter). Unfortunately, as we move to more Metaverse-focused experiences with more players, more latency changes, and more dynamic scenarios, these solutions degrade. It's difficult to predict a dozen players in a cohesive and accurate manner and then 'roll them back in a non-disruptive manner. It is better to simply unplug a slow player. While there may be several participants in a video conference, only one is relevant at any given time, resulting in 'core' delay.

In a game, getting the right information from all participants is critical, and latency exacerbates the problem.

Low latency isn't an issue for most games. While Hearthstone and Words with Friends are both turn-based and asynchronous games, Honour of Kings and Candy Crush do not necessitate pixel-perfect or millisecond-precise inputs. Low latency is only required for fast-paced games such as Fortnite, Call of Duty, and Forza Motorsport. These games are profitable, but they account for only a small portion of the total games market in terms of titles created – and even less in terms of total gaming time.

While the Metaverse isn't a fast-paced AAA game, its social nature and desired importance necessitate low latency. In human conversation, minor facial movements are critical, and we are acutely aware of minor errors and synchronisation difficulties (hence the uncanny valley problem in CGI). It is also necessary for the ubiquity of social products. Consider what it would be like if FaceTime or Facebook only worked if you were within 500 miles of your friends or family. You could also limit yourself to doing it only at home. And, in the virtual world, we'll need much more than just extra bandwidth to tap into international or long-distance labour.

Unfortunately, of all network characteristics, latency is the most difficult and time-consuming to address. Part of the issue stems from the fact that, as previously stated, only a small number of services and applications require ultra-low latency delivery. This limits the economic case for any network operator or latency-focused content-delivery network (CDN) – and fundamental physics rules are already posing a challenge to the business case.

Traveling 11,000–12,500 kilometres from New York City to Tokyo or Mumbai takes 40–45 minutes.

This meets all of the low-latency requirements. Despite the fact that fibre optic cable makes up the majority of the internet backbone, it falls 30% short of the speed of light

186

because it is rarely in a vacuum (+ loss is typically 3.5 dB/km). Copper and coaxial cables suffer from even worse distance latency degradation and bandwidth constraints, resulting in increased congestion and delivery delays.

Nonetheless, these cables continue to account for the vast majority of those found in residential and commercial building interiors, as well as in neighbourhoods.

Furthermore, none of these wires are in the path of a crow's flight. The "internet backbone" is a loose federation of private networks, none of which can deliver a data packet properly (or have the incentive to trade off stretches to a competitor with a faster segment or two). As a result, the networking distance between two servers, or between a server and a client, may be greater than their geographical distance. Furthermore, network congestion may cause data to be routed less directly in order to ensure consistent and continuous delivery, rather than decreasing latency. As a result, the average latency between New York and Tokyo is more than four times the time it takes light to travel between the two cities, and the average latency between New York and Mumbai is four to six times the time it takes light to travel between the two cities.

Any cable-based infrastructure update or relay is extremely costly and complicated, particularly if the goal is to reduce geographic distance. It also necessitates extensive regulatory/government approval, which is usually required at multiple levels. Wireless, on the other hand, is much easier to repair. And 5G certainly helps, as it reduces 4G latency by 20–40ms on average (and promises as little as 1ms). This, however, only helps with the last few hundred metres of data transfer.

After your data arrives at the tower, you return to standard backbones.

SpaceX's satellite Internet constellation corporation, Starlink, promises to bring high-bandwidth, low-latency internet to the United States and, eventually, the rest of the world. This, however, does not account for extremely low latency, particularly over long distances. While Starlink has a trip time of 18–35 milliseconds from your house to the satellite and back, data must travel from New York to Los Angeles and back. After all, relaying through multiple satellites is required. In some cases, Starlink makes travel times longer. For example, the distance from New York to Philadelphia in a straight line is approximately 100 miles, and possibly 125 miles by cable, but over 700 miles when travelling to a low-orbit satellite and back down.

Furthermore, on cloudy days, fiber-optic cable has a lower loss rate than light transmitted through the environment. Densely populated urban areas are also noisy, which makes them vulnerable to interference. In 2020, Elon Musk stated that Starlink is focused on "the hardest-to-serve clients who [telecommunications firms] would otherwise have difficulty reaching." This way, rather than enhancing those who are already present, it welcomes newcomers to the Metaverse.

Completely new technologies, business lines, and services are being developed to meet the increased demand for real-time bandwidth applications. Subspace (Disclosure: portfolio company), for example, deploys hardware across hundreds of cities to create 'weather maps' for low latency network pathfinding, runs a networking stack that incorporates the needs of a low latency application with the many third-parties that comprise this path, and has also built an optical network that splices across various fibre networks to shorten the distance between servers and minimise the use of non-fiber c.

Fastly, on the other hand, offers a CDN that prioritises low-latency apps over delivery reliability and bandwidth.

The company claims that a software application can clear and replace all cached content across all of these clusters globally in 150ms and that it can cache and accelerate individual blockchain transactions in real-time using a "infrastructure-as-code" approach that allows clients to customise nearly every aspect of the company's edge-computing clusters.

Reliability

Dependability is a self-evident concept. Our ability to transition to virtual work and education is dependent on maintaining consistent service quality. This includes the overall uptime as well as other factors such as download/upload bandwidth and latency consistency. Much of what follows may come as a surprise to many people who 'live online' these days—Netflix typically streams in 1080p or even 4K. Netflix, on the other hand, employs reliability solutions that aren't appropriate for games or Metaverse-specific applications.

Non-live video providers, such as Netflix, receive all video files for months before making them available to viewers. This allows them to perform in-depth analysis to reduce (or compress) file sizes by examining frame data to determine what information can be removed. For example, if a viewer's connection bandwidth drops, Netflix's algorithms will 'watch' a

189

scene with blue skies and determine whether 500 different shades of blue can be simplified to 200, 50, or 25. The streamer's algorithms account for this on a per-scene basis, recognising that scenes with dialogue can withstand more compression than scenes with fast-paced action. This is known as multipass encoding. As previously stated, Netflix uses extra bandwidth to transfer content to a user's device before it is needed, so the end-user is unaffected if there is a brief drop in connectivity or increase in latency.

Furthermore, Netflix will pre-load content at local nodes, so the latest Stranger Things episode is only a few blocks away when you request it. This isn't an option for live video or data, which, as previously stated, must be delivered faster. This is why cloud-streaming one gigabyte of Stadia is more difficult than cloud-streaming one gigabyte of Netflix.

While Metaverse's goal isn't inherently competitive, we should think of it as raising the bar for all aspects of networking — latency, reliability/resilience, and bandwidth — to the level of AAA multiplayer games. It doesn't matter how powerful your equipment is (see hardware and computing) if it can't get all of the data it needs quickly.